Rainbows But Not Unicorns

My Adoption Truth

By Mae Claire

This book was written using Time New Roman, size 12 font.

Names of people, places and particular events have been changed to protect those who are still living. This is a work of nonfiction by the author in the form of blogs/stream of conscious writing, and general thought-provoking outbursts.

Cover Drawing: F. Carroll

Title Drawing: F. Carroll

*Italicized dates under a chapter = blog post

Self-Publishing via Lulu by Mae Claire

ISBN: 978-1-365-04529-5

©Mae Claire 2016
Rainbows but not Unicorns: My Adoption Truth
malinecarroll@gmail.com

Podcast: Evol365.podbean.com

Blog: solifegoeson.com

Facebook page: Nooma Consulting: Understanding the
Complexities of Adoption

Follow me on twitter: @noomaconsulting

Introduction

Hey, I am a Haitian adoptee telling you my story through a compilation of essays, blogs and outrageous outbursts. It is my story and my truth and I own this reality.

Please do not attempt to read this book as if you are reading a novel because it is not one!

This book is for everyone in the adoption and foster care triad. My hope is that as an adoptee you are able to find a connection. As an adoptive or foster parent, you read what my lips have to say, and hear what my heart cries out. As a birth parent, you understand that you are valued and loved.

Without you, I would not be able to speak my truth.

For my Mother

who felt she had

no choice but to give

me away;

    hoping against all hope that I would survive.

        I have mom. I have.

        R.I.P Yolette

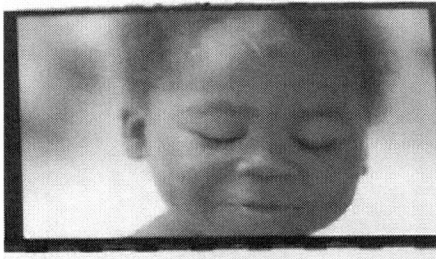

AM-Adoptive Mom/mother

AP-Adoptive Parent

AS-Adoptive sibling

COC-Child of Color

FF-Foster Family

FP-Foster Parent

KOC-Kid of Color

PAP-Potential Adoptive Parent

POC-Person of Color

RAD-Reactive Attachment Disorder

TRA-Trans Racial Adoption/Adoptee

WAF-White Adoptive Father

WAM-White Adoptive Mother

WAP-White Adoptive Parent

Table of Contents

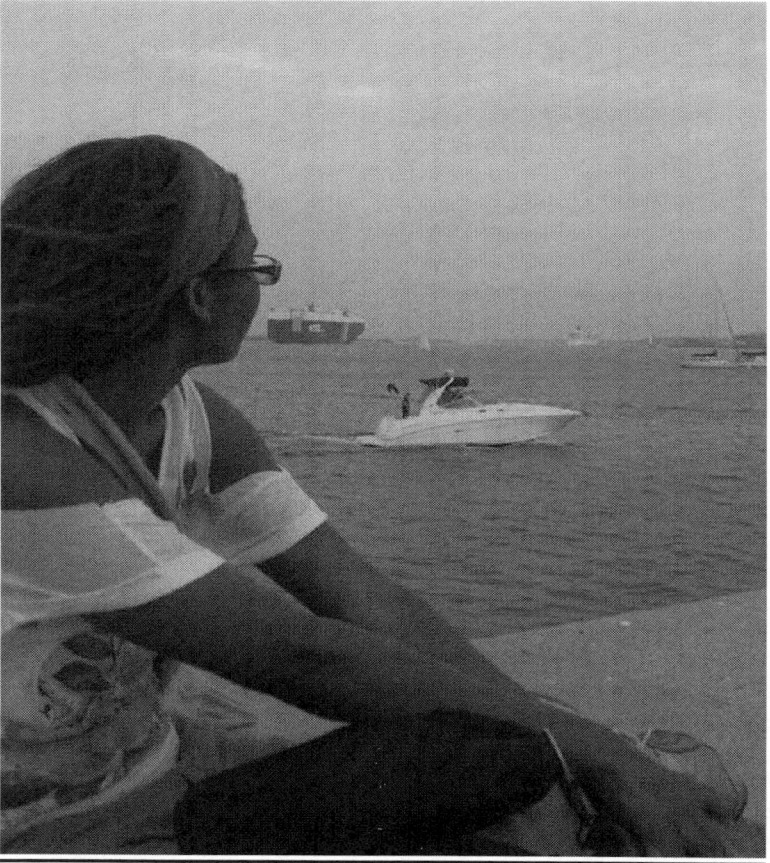

"Here's the thing. If you want a transracial family, marry a person of color. DO NOT use adopted children to create your "perfect" family; leaving adoptees feeling responsible for making your life colorful." Jenny S.

"Different" Love

Parents, take a second to clear your browsing data.

I was supposed to start this podcast at around 1pm but it is now around 1:55 and I'm late for my own podcast. My computer was having trouble performing all of the tasks I was trying to force it to do. So I shut it down and I restarted it and it still was not connecting or registering that I needed it to do something right now…. right this minute.

Sometimes an adoptee can feel like the computer a parent is using. You want us to say, feel and do something immediately, you want to give us more information than we can handle at one time, and at the wrong stage. You want us to be like you….and take happy pictures, and smile…and be part of the family…. but sometimes what you are asking us to do forces us to shut down.

And when we shut down, we just need you to listen and be there. Don't try to "restart" us. Sometimes adoptive parents (APs), we need you to mentally *clear your browsing data.* Everything YOU know, or what YOU have read, or what YOU are trying to do…. sometimes, they just don't apply…so it is not US who need a "restart" (we have had many already), it is YOU.

This morning, I awoke to my wife telling me about this article that asks a very interesting question. It asks whether adoptive mothers/parents love their biological children more than their adopted children. And so many people were offended and others chose to reflect. The article is called: "A Different Kind of Love" by Kate Hilpern.*

Here is my reflection as an adoptee.

Yes: The answer to this question is YES. For me, for my lived experience. For who I am as a person.

Connected

I was sick when I was given up for adoption, so there was already a bond that was severed.

Bond # 1: Utero
1. It's been proven over and over that the bond that is created in the mother's womb is the first and most important bond that will be had and will begin to shape the mind of a child.
2. The voices; the mother's voice, the father's voice, the nutrients being received, the nutrients being denied. If the mother is stressed out, the baby feels it.
3. If the mother plays music, the baby feels the vibrations. Drugs, alcohol, violence; all of these things are felt in the womb.

Bond # 2: Mother
1. Once a child is born, they create another bond, with the hope of staying connected to what they had in the womb.
2. A child who stays with the biological family, recognizes voices and is allowed to continue down this path of familiarity.
3. A child who is adopted has to readjust their brain. No longer do they feel what they heard, or felt or sensed. They are no longer

familiar with what they had bonded with from Day 1.

4. No longer do they recognize what they held so dear for 9 months. It is like going from A to Z within seconds.

Take a second and think about something you have never been a part of before. And now put yourself there. How do you feel? What do you see? Would there be people you recognize?

My mother (Yolette), gave me up probably at around 3 months of age. This means that I had already felt a bond and I was already connected. I spent 9 months in her womb, and I spent three months in her arms. I spent a year in full contact with this person who would later give me up. Touching, feeling, knowing that this togetherness was what I wanted, what any child would want. I knew I was loved. How could I not have been loved? I was alive. I was breathing (sick, but breathing), I was doted on. I ate, slept, and was held by my mother, day in and day out. She loved me. I was hers. She was mine.

And then I got sick and she did not have the means to take care of me. I didn't know I was sick. I was told I was sick; I was told I cried a lot. There was something that was not right. This bond was being lost bit by bit. She was scared, and she didn't know what to do. I was 3 months old…. she was young, but had other children to feed. I was now one extra mouth to feed, body to care for and medical bill to pay.

But things were perfect before I was sick, and then I got sick. Now, this bond starts to shift. I can feel the tension, I can feel the pain, I can feel the fear she has in her voice; it shakes, it trembles. I can feel it change in the way she holds me now....in a more fragile way.... she keeps me closer to her body...for fear of me falling, me dying.

Abandoned

There it is now.... that bond is breaking and my brain is reshaping itself already. My brain, even as a baby is clicking on the hazard lights. Something is not right (I'm thinking in my mind) but I'm a baby so I have no idea really.

And then she hands me over to the authorities. Hoping, praying that this new place will give me food, and drink and take care of me medically. Hoping that I won't fall through the cracks.

New voices, new sounds, the touch of their hands is not the same as my mothers. Their breath smells different, the side of their face looks different. I no longer hear the rest of the siblings. I hear other kids...lots of them. They are loud. Some are crying, some are laughing. And I'm still a baby laying on my back.

I freeze-now, my brain is taking on a new formation. That bond I once had with my mom is no longer there, and will no longer ever be there because she is no longer there.

A dark room became my new home. I open my eyes and see darkness. I close my eyes to sleep and there is still darkness. I can't even differentiate between day and night because they have kept me in this room, the size of a closet. Me, and several others.

We were many. We were the ones who probably would not survive. We were sick, we had defects, we were not cared for.

We went days and weeks without seeing sunlight, we went days and weeks without food. We were bathing in our own filth, and we ate each other's. I was damaged goods-who would want me now?

Adopted

And then the new orphanage I was in took better care of me and some white lady from the US wanted to be my new mother. I only wanted my real mother. But she gave me up, so why would I really want her back? Maybe it was her voice, or the way she made me feel safe. Maybe it was the way she spoke to me, the way she held me, the way she sang to me in Creole. Maybe it was the familiarity that I missed.

This woman didn't look anything like me. But she was nice at first. She was pretty. Long dark hair, lovely smile. She had a rough touch. I was afraid of that from the beginning. I know this now because of the way she would hold me. She lacked love.

So they fostered me for a bit, I was around 3 now. They looked different. I was always curious, but I was never in love. I couldn't bond with them. It was impossible for me to bond with them because I was damaged goods.

My mother had given me up, and now for me, that equaled I was not good enough. So I learned to accept what was around me in the orphanage. I knew when I was supposed to go back into the closet with my other companions. We must have played, slept, and just existed.

They took me to America, they showed me candy land; a land filled with milk and honey. But they also had another child with them. She was white. I was the Black Sheep and she was the Golden Girl. Prettier, smarter and always smiling. I never smiled.

My new "mom" would pinch me if I did not smile…she wanted us to look like a perfect family in the pictures. They were the White Parents saving the Black disabled child-yep, that was Me.

In Nancy Verner's book *The Primal Wound: Understanding the Adopted Child*, she states that all children who are separated from their mother suffer a trauma that will affect their bond with their new parents, regardless of the age at which they enter that new family. This view is 100% on the money in my case because:

1. *I was incapable* of going back and forming a bond no matter who wanted to love me. I was incapable because by the time I was 7 years old, my brain was no longer as much of a sponge as it is when you are young and open and receptive.
2. *I don't recall ever having love* for my new family. I just had anger, jealousy and sometimes even rage. I had so many questions that they could never answer. I

was restricted in so many ways that my sisters were not.

3. *I was treated very differently*. One example of being treated differently was being put at the top of the bunk bed. I had just been adopted and they put me at the top of the bunk bed. It is more dangerous to be put at the top of the bunk bed…. but their biological daughter got the bottom. I rolled out of the top one day after having a traumatic dream and I split my head. I still have the scar to prove it.

Everything my sister wanted, she would get (food, toys, money, fun outings)

I had to have my sister ask for stuff for me, so that they would give it to her, so that she could later give it to me.

4. I was never able to connect with them, which left me feeling even more jealous and mad at myself.

The experience of not being able to connect is multi layered. This onion needs to be peeled back to get to the root of the issue. And my APs never cared to peel it. They continued to see me as the difficult child and they saw her as the loving, quiet and submissive child.

I could never love them. And I never liked them. Yes, they fed and clothed me and put me in school (possibly to keep up their outward persona and a "good" reputation). They even sent me off to college. But as an adult, knowing that it was my grandfather who paid for our education, I am left to wonder if they would have put me in college in the first place.

For example, for years I had been asking them to help me with my master's program and they continued to refuse. But when my sister went down the wrong road, and almost failed undergraduate, they offered to put her through medical school. Medical school is expensive, and yet maintained they "never had the money" to put me through a master's program.

I knew they loved her more because she was the easier child. She was the one who would do whatever they said. She was the first to smile in every picture. Her hair was easier to do; she was thinner than I…. you see, she reflected them. There is something about a biological child that forces an AP to love them more…and so many will say "NO, NOT I," but the truth is…. when you are willing to do one thing for one child and not for the other, the word "different" translates to "more" in the eyes of the adoptee.

When an AP says they have a different love for their adopted child, they are really saying they are not *connecting* with them the way they *connect* with their biological child. And for an adoptee, this translates to "they love them more."

No AP ever wants to think that love is so layered. Those who think love has no layers, and has no bounds are living the rainbows and unicorn's fairytale.

What I liked about this article is that the AP's lived experience with their adopted child is so real…and some were so honest. This is a very important conversation to have. This NEEDS to be had.

The word "different" equates to levels or hierarchy to an adoptee. They already know that they are different. They already know they don't fit in because of so many factors. They already know that their previous life was cut short and they have been "given a second chance." The last thing they need is to feel that the love they are receiving is different from the love the others are receiving.

APs, hear me out! We are not judging your parenting styles. We are judging how you react to your adopted children when they are sharing from their heart. Does what they say to you matter? Do their feelings matter? Do you spend a bit more time listening to one child more than the other? What are your adopted children saying and are you listening to them?

The article was AP-centric; I agree with that (someone pointed that out on the thread). But the issue is not the AP's, the issue is the way the adopted children feel, regardless of the effort being put in.

For me, I was damaged goods. I say this because so many of my bonding experience had been cut short at such a young age. Thus bonding has always been difficult to nearly impossible for me to do. And after continuous psychological, physical, and emotional abuse bonding was non-existent.

And the layers continue and the complexity extends itself. In order to effectively connect with my child, I must incorporate things I never experienced as a child. So I am learning….it is as though I'm starting from square one.

The tension an adoptee has in a home with biological kids will always be strained because of the bonding component. Adoptive parents who claim to love *equally* are not only lying to themselves, but they are lying to their children; on both sides.

There is a unique feeling that all mothers experience when they give birth to a child. But when they give birth to their child, and the child comes from them, there is either a connect or a disconnect that happens. There is a physical disconnect (placenta), but then there is a bond that is formed or not formed. Either way, there is no denying the womb-closeness. *ALL BABIES HAVE EXPERIENCED THE WOMB CLOSENESS.*

I think oftentimes with adoption; APs fail to recognize that the WOMB CLOSENESS was created with their adopted child. They fail to fully appreciate the womb's power in the lives of their adopted children. But undeniably understand the power in their biological children. They dismiss the birthmother's experience. They neglect to realize that these children are biological children too and somewhere, at some point, the fact that they are biological, mattered and matters to their real mom.

This experience is life-changing.

I urge all of you listening with your hearts and reading, to really think about what I have said here. This is my lived experience and am realizing more and more that it is not just me who feels this way. Find a way to get out of your own heads, and hold the hand of your adopted child, walk with them as they feel less love...because this is how you show them that you LOVE.

I'm Warning YOU!

For many of you reading, you are probably thinking I am anti-adoption. I am. And yet, I adopted my daughter in 2015 after living with her for almost 9 years. I am anti-adoption because parents don't know how to parent children that are not related to them. There are parents who can't even parent their own children, so imagine someone who does not "belong" to them.

So why don't you stop reading this right now? I've made this the second chapter of this book on purpose. Can you get through this? It is not an easy read and there are really no "feel good" moments. Because it is my truth, and if you don't like it, you can return the book and I'll give it to someone who wants to hear real components of the adoption triad. I'm not here to make money off and I'm not here to acquire fame. I'm here to *save* you before you completely fuck up your minority children who will NEVER receive the (white) privilege you have had all your life. I am here to let you know that adoption sucks on so many levels. I want to tell you that when you take a child away from their birth-ness, you create a huge void that will NEVER EVER be fully filled. It's like making pizza; we can never quite get the dough to fluff the way we want it to.

That is how we adoptees feel. And for those adoptees who say "my adoptive family was great, all the time…and I never had any issues," congratulations! Write a book about it, sell millions of copies, give a book talk (which I will not attend) and we can all go home. For those adoptees who feel that "I'm being too harsh" or for those APs who think "man, how dare she point out exactly what I didn't want her to point out…" the dough has not risen yet. It's still in the oven, about to fully form into what you *never really expected.*

Adoption is complicated! There are so many layers. Think about a girl raised without a mother, or a father. Think about a boy who was raised only by one parent and spends his entire life wondering where the "other half" went. Adoption includes these cases to its FULLEST extent. We are not only missing one parent; we are missing both.... all.... all of our people are no longer part of what we once knew. And then to top it all off, we are given *new* parents who expect us to fit in immediately. We are introduced to people who don't look a thing like us. We are introduced to people who will hurt us, rape us, lie to us, steal from us, hate us because we are not doing it right. These people will fail to make us fully part of them because we didn't live up to their expectations.

We are also introduced to people who have no fucking idea what they are doing but their love for us is so strong they go to any length to make sure we stay connected. There are not many of these people. But the few are absolutely beautiful. And for whatever reason we are introduced to them, we take the next step and learn, albeit slowly, to trust that they won't abandon us too.

I got to meet my real mom several times when I was really little. I don't remember the encounters; I only have pictures to prove it. But why was I meeting someone I spiritually, emotionally, physically and vaginally came from? Why was the term "meet" ever used? I had a connection with her in the womb. We are not meeting for the first time; we are just reuniting. But yet the word "meeting" was always used, as if I was cut off from her…and I was.

And yet, as an adult, connecting with my real family has felt like "meeting" them for the first time. I don't know them, I know we are related, I know we have similar physical characteristics, I know that at one point, we were a family, and now, I don't know who they are.

Some of you APs will care enough to make sure your Kids of Color stay connected, but others will not give a shit. For me, my parents didn't give a shit.

I found out a day or so ago that my parents had a lot more to do with the unethicalness of my adoption than I had thought. Besides having the name of a dead person, and besides not really knowing anything about my roots, they don't care to tell me how the adoption *really* happened. Maybe they are afraid?

It is crucial that you do not make your adoption within the home "closed." The birth mom may choose not to be in contact, but you MUST give your child(ren) the opportunity and freedom to question, wonder, and search for their first, birth, and real parents.

Your children were ripped from what they knew; now you owe it to them to untie the knots you so tightly tied for your comfort, safety, and "their" protection.

I'm not an expert on many things, but what I do know is that I am an expert on my own lived experiences. And the most interesting thing about all of that is that it is not just MY lived experience, it is the lived experience of so many children who are adopted by white families, or who are adopted in general. It is the lived experience that make us feel connected and yet so disconnected from society. It is the thought that we were and are never good enough and that we will never match up. It is the social construct that tells us that we should have been a bit *lighter* to get that boyfriend, or that girlfriend. It's the feeling from the new parents that we are somehow less. It's the idea that we were a "gift" from God…like a stork who drops off its delivery on the door step. It's the hurtful deep-seeded belief that we could possibly be sent back because our behavior is too unruly…or we failed to attach properly, or we can't find love. These are the things I share in common with others who have these lived experiences.

So many people tell me that I am an angry adoptee. They are right! But I'm also an adoptee who is trying to make a difference through my writing, my reading of other's writing, my webinars, my talks, and my books. I spend countless hours on the phone with APs, adoptees, and also first mothers. My desire is to listen, and by using my lived experiences, tell them how I've grown and become the person I am today.

My hope for you as adoptive parents, is that you find the system unsettling. My desire is that you find anger…so much anger that it drives you to change the system: foster care, domestic adoption, and international adoption. My hope is for you to be disturbed enough to take action. *You* are the problem but have the power to be the solution.

Our lived experience is what your child may be or become one day, and in order to be by their side, you need to read the hard stuff.

Is there a rainbow at the end of this tunnel? I think you will need to answer that for yourself. And as you figure it out, you can decide whether you want to walk or ride the unicorn into the fading mist and fog that colors everything equally.

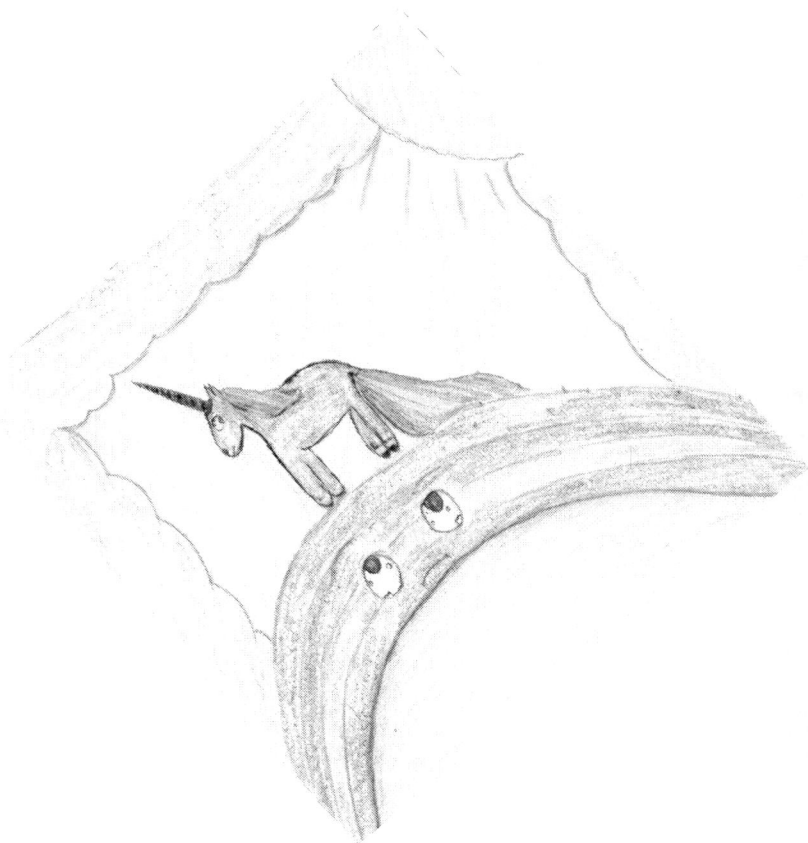

ANGER

Christmas

Christmas is never a time of Joy for me because it reminds me of so much hurt. Maybe I smiled in the pictures, but that really does not mean I was happy. My a-mom (Lydia), preferably known as *Loca* or *crazy*, forced us to smile in pictures. We were never allowed to have an actual candid moment because she wanted us to reflect her and what she has supposedly done for us.

How many adoptees out there can relate to this?

I am an adult now and thinking about Christmas makes me sick. If it were not for our 13-year-old daughter, we would *not* have a tree nor would we celebrate Christmas.

It is just a day.

Another day of sadness.

Another day of confusion.

Another day of asking "Why."

A stream of hate texts, mail, and phone calls came from my adoptive family after I published my book *A Failed Adoption: Who is Your Larimar?* But their reaction was not immediately after, it was actually a couple years later when the book gained a bit of footing. I had introduced one of my kids' books to a family friend, and they liked it so much they decided to look into what else I had written. They came across the above mentioned book and it made them question everything they knew about my adoptive family.

It was not about my book; it was about my AP's image. They cut me off, they cut me out of their world.

When I was three years old, they cut a space in their heart for me and now that space has been filled with anger and hatred toward me.

I never created space for them.

There is something about adoption that is very hard to understand for many white adoptive parents or adoptive parents in general. Children don't ask to be adopted, nor do they ask to have their entire world turned upside-down.

Children don't look through a catalogue to pick their "perfect" family. It is quite the opposite. Children are not asked if they want to be part of something that will alter their lives forever. They are thrown into a situation they have no control over. One minute they are poor and the next minute, they are in a living room where there is more than they could ever imagine. Christmas was like that for me.

Growing up surrounded by material things, surrounded by many white Santas and white angels and white, white, white. Christmas was tough for me. The worst Christmas I remember was when I was molested. We were at my aunt Cindy's in New Hampshire. I remember it quite well.

My APs brought a foster son of theirs to the US to celebrate Christmas. This was the same foster sibling who had started molesting me when I was about 8 or 9 years old. I had no clue what was going on, all I knew was that whatever he was doing felt strange, and good at the same time. And that I couldn't tell anyone, that it was wrong somehow. So my APs bring him to the US with us and on Christmas, all the children slept by the tree and he slept beside me and molested me.

I can't get that image and feeling out of my head.
Every Christmas brings back these memories.

Am I Ungrateful, or do I just not give a SHIT?

November 24th 2015

I was one of those people who stopped giving a shit. I stopped caring that I was adopted, that I had a "home," that I had a bed to sleep in at night, that I had an "education." That I had food.

I stopped caring.

I started cutting.

I started smacking myself in the face. I started skipping meals and then sneaking food from the fridge in the middle of the night.

I stopped caring.

I became numb because caring would mean bowing down to my AP's insane rules, regulations and idea of who I was.

I stopped caring because the white bio kids didn't have to care; they were not made to feel as though they had to care. So what made me different? According to my APs, I was ungrateful, unthankful…and all the other "uns."

Am I raising this kind of child? After adoptees grow up, we reflect on our life and how we were raised. We ask many questions and receive few answers.

We go on long searches for our birth parents that span a lifetime.

Our search starts in the womb and ends in the tomb.

Sometimes we find them, sometimes we don't. Sometimes when we find them we feel more alive, and sometimes we find them and we want to die all over again.

Am I raising this kind of child? The transracial adoption group (TRA) is an amazing group that is constantly challenging adoptive parents, adoptees and first parents to reflect, share and create a space for real unadulterated love where there may not have been. It was through this group that I really started to learn what my real issues were. One of my many issues was that I learned to not give a shit!

Raising children is hard in general. Throw in the mix the following: a child who was abandoned not just once but many times, a child who does not match your race, a child with disabilities. This is all a recipe for disaster. At some point, there will be an inevitable combustion. Either an internal combustion or an external combustion will follow.

Let me explain how I see this:

An internal combustion happens when the outsider (usually the adoptee) hides how they really feel. Then one day they write a book. And not just write a book, but writes several books. One book is an "I hate this fucking life and I hate you and all white people book" and then the next book is about "How I am so sorry for hating you." And then by the time book three comes out, the audience can hear a pin drop.

Yep, that is me, that is my life. And not only books, but we blog, and we angry blog, and we sex blog, and we whip nae nae blog, and we give advice blog, and we take advice blog and we epiphany blog but rarely do we happy blog.

An external combustion happens when the caregivers react to the internal combustion by the adoptee. This looks HORRIBLE let me tell ya! Because you can have many different caregivers/APs. Some of them really do love you, and some of them really don't.

Some of them will talk to you about race, and change

and assimilation,

and love,

and joy,

and peace,

and flowers.

But others will talk to you about *their* race, *their* change, *their* assimilation (having to deal with you), *their* love and what they think it looks like, and *their* joy (and how you are ruining it), *their* peace (and how they can't find it because of you) and *their* flowers…. because *their* shit apparently smells like flowers.

Am I raising this kind of child? I'm trying to raise a grateful child and be a good a-mother at the same time, but it is extremely hard. I don't like to make excuses but I do believe that your past follows you forever and ever. And sometimes church makes it sound so easy. "Give it to Jesus…. give it up today." And sometimes people dismiss your feelings "look, it's not that bad," and sometimes the sun tricks you by coming up the next day when it promised it would not shine and you could retreat to your death hole. Sometimes we feel forced to say "tomorrow is new and it will not be repeated."

Am I raising this kind of child? Raising kids is like working at the bottom and finally making your way to the top to find out that it comes with a whole new set of rules and regulations each step of the way. And guess what my friends, no child can be raised the same way…. No maam! My 20-year-old is so different from my 12-year-old, not because of the 8-year age difference, but because of the way their brains function. My 20-year-old would not take *no* for an answer so we started saying "yes" with the word "when" attached to it. "Y*es*, you can go to the party and get smashing drunk *when* you are 18 and out of the house" (that one was always my favorite!) But this 12-year-old…. shiiiiiiiiiiiiieeeeeeeeeeeettttttttttt!!! It doesn't seem to matter what we take away or reward her with, she DON'T GIVE A SHIT.

When it gets to the point of not caring, have I messed it up? I'd say no, I have not because there is a fine line between not caring, and being ungrateful. As a child, at the heart of it all, I was so grateful, and thankful for being alive even though I didn't give a shit that it was with them or because of them. It is hard to explain. It is like we appreciate the fact that we exist, but then we don't care that it was our APs who supposedly "called" us into existence.

Are we raising our kids to feel that they need to be so grateful that they start to really not care that they are part of our family? Are we trying too hard to teach them to NOT be *ungrateful* that they start to not G-A-S?

I'm very careful (thanks to my transracial adoption group) of how I approach gratefulness. And when I use it, I make sure it is not tied to adoption, or foster care. I also do my best to not pull the "guilt" trip on my kids but because I am human, I slip and have to be reminded not to follow in my scary AP's footsteps. But are we avoiding the word grateful so much that we are actually creating kids who don't give a shit?

I had an incident and I feel I handled it somewhat appropriately. My daughter kept repeating the same infraction over and over again. I explained to her that it feels as though she does not care about what we say because she keeps doing the same stuff over and over. I then proceeded to explain that I felt she was so spoiled and had everything, that this may be contributing to her "not caring" attitude. I pointed to the pantry and told her to look inside of it. I told her that I knew entire families who lived inside a room not much bigger than the pantry. I explained to her that both her and I can't imagine living this way because we have everything we need. I continued to explain that the family did everything in the pantry: cooked, slept, homework, watched TV, used the bathroom. The amount of space and resources were so limited.

As I spoke to her I had an *Aha* Moment.

She has too much.

And in her mind, when she loses one thing, she can get it again either through grandma, the cousins, or her uncles or even us; her parents. She has too much. I decided to simplify her room. I took makeup, jewelry and the mirror out of her room. I removed things from her room that she didn't need. Like, she didn't need 5 pillows…. that is a luxury. The more she had, the harder it was for her to concentrate on homework, and keep the room neat.

As parents we are to teach empathy, love, and joy. I don't believe kids just have it, they see it and they try to make sense of it and apply it to their lives. If our kids have too much, it is so hard for them to see what living a simple life consists of. When you live a simple life, and enjoy what you have around you, (including family and friends), you start to understand what it means to really be thankful and have gratitude.

APs, it is not about showering your adoptive kids with things they may never have had.

You do not owe adoptees a "better" life.

They did not ask for this life you gave them.

This idea is traumatic for the triad. I have seen many families waiting at the airport with gifts and teddy bears and stuff that the kids don't need or want. They have gone so long without it, what makes us think they need it now? Things that may comfort the western world may not be the same thing that comforts an adoptee. It is not about giving them their own room, their own bed, their own computer.... their own bathroom. It is not about making them feel guilty for not saying thank you. It is about watching them say thank you because they want to-because they are starting to understand what caring really is about. It is about listening to them say "I love you" not because you gave them shit...but because you gave them another path.

Am I raising that kind of child-one who will not give a shit because she has too much shit or one who will care because being grateful is not about guilt?

It's about that fine line.

Don't create trauma where it does not belong.

Jesus H Christ!

As a blogger I've been asked many times whether I am a Christian or a believer in Christ. The Christian religion has been used against me by my APs and my a-mother always claimed to be the mediator between God and myself. She told me constantly that *God told her*, or that she *prayed and Jesus told her* to do something.

I was a kid, so I believed her of course. It would be rude for me not to take every word she was saying to heart.

And then this happened:

I was about 10 years old and we had a huge painting done by Michelangelo on our wall. It was the one with the Archangel, partially nude. If you stared at the painting long enough, you would think that the angel was floating towards you. At the bottom right, there was something written in burnt wax or black ink. My name was written there. Poorly scribbled and yet, it was clear that my actual name had been deliberately written on this expensive collectible.

I knew for a fact it was not me. Why, in my right mind would I want to draw on a painting that did not belong to me? Of course I was a child though. Kids do that, they doodle, they draw, they make messes.

My children decided one day that they would stand on the bed and use permanent marker to draw on the walls. They were 4 and 3 years old and they were so excited that their masterpiece was almost done. I say almost done because I caught them right before that "T" was crossed and that "I" was dotted. I was upset. They got spankings because I was not happy with what they had done. But they were kids. I saw it, I watched them get excited when I walked into the room, as if to show me how cool they were to be professional drawers. But that is the difference;

I saw it.

My APs did not see anything. My a-mother promised that God had told her that I had done it. I was grounded for about a month and I remember not being allowed to eat any sweets like the other kids. That is when I realized that there must be something wrong with this religion they are telling me about and forcing me to be a part of.

But we were not "religious" per se, we were just the type who had all these strange rituals. They never forced us to have Christ come into our hearts but they did force us to pray at the table, out loud. And then they had the nerve to compare who prayed better than whom. It was weird. The whole thing felt cult-like.

And yet somehow, I survived. I survived this crazy Jesus stuff. I, oddly enough, am a believer in something because something saved me from this craziness.

I identify with something greater than myself.

An "Ok" Memory

I do not have much recollection of what it was like when I was a kid. I feel that I tend to only remember the bad things that have happened to me. Call me a negative person, but the "good" times seemed to be few and far between.

Let's go back about 25 years. I was about 10 years old and my a-mother was throwing my 10th birthday. We had this huge backyard with a couple swings, a twisty rope, and a tree house. I remember never being able to go into the tree house because I was always too tall, or too fat. My biggest fear was I would step on a piece of unhooked wood and go tumbling down. The treehouse was also constantly riddled with bees and I had a horrible bee allergy. So I avoided the tree house at all cost.

My "friends" were all there. I say friends because they were people who came to visit ever-so-often. But as for real friends, no. I didn't have many. My white sister Nora, on the other hand was also 10 and was super popular in school and around town. She was blonde, with beautiful green eyes. She was the person all the middle school boys looked at. To top it, she was also smart. Not like overly intelligent smart, but she never studied for tests. That was what we called smart back in those days. If you don't study, and yet know the answers, people thought you were a genius. I just always thought she was a good guesser.

The yard had many trees. The trees' branches seemed to stretch for miles on end. If you were not careful, and decided to go running around in the yard, it was very likely you would trip on one of the overgrown roots.
My 5th grade party. Wow! What a great event. At least it should have been. I was really around twelve years of age

but my a-parents did not really know how old I was because when I was adopted, the paper work was all screwed up. (This was what I was told as a child. I now know better.)

Oh yes, and did I mention that we were not only celebrating my 10th birthday, but also the birthday of all the rest of my siblings? My a-parents were cheap. Kill two birds with one stone. There were five of us and instead of giving a party to each kid, (you know, to make them feel special), they threw it all together. So here's to mine, and my four other sibling's birthday bash.

We had a piñata. We almost always had one of those. My a-mother would hand make it with papier-mâché. I remember being super young and watching her dip the newspaper into the glue goo. I can remember also helping her pop the balloons once the papier-mâché had dried up. There was never any noise, except for a low hissing sound; the sound of the balloon losing air.

The piñata hung above the tree that held our tree house together. It dangled on the very end of the strongest branch possible. It was always painted, colored and decorated to its fullest extent. This would really be the only party anyone would have all year so they had to deck it out real nicely.

The broomstick sat at the base of the tree house, just waiting for us to take it by its neck and use it as some weapon of mass destruction. Right before the party was over, and after we had eaten the cake made from scratch, we would mosey on down to the big tree area and grab the broomstick. All the kids would get into one single file line. There were about 25 of us; five friends per child celebrating their birthday. It was always a grand and glorious occasion.

I batted last. Always last because I was the "biggest" one there. My a-mother never ceased to remind me that I was the bigger and fatter one in the family. "Are you sure you need to eat that Claire? Does your body need one more piece of chicken?" I couldn't explain to her how often I was hungry. My body never seemed to get enough food. I was growing, and she didn't understand that my body was not finished growing like hers was.

She was 5'4, weighing about 110 pounds. A beautiful woman really. Dark brown hair waving in the wind as we drove past one of her many gift stores she had set up in a tiny town called Sosna. Her eyes were a dark blue shade. Her lips, I was always mesmerized by the shape of her lips and her high cheekbones. The way she walked exemplified authority, power, and strength. A true feminist with many flaws.

When she spoke, everyone stopped, turned, and listened to what she had to say. The problem was she was always speaking; she couldn't shut up. But she was my idol. I looked up to her with respect and pure hatred at the same time. I wanted to be like her in physicality, but nothing like her in spirit. Her beauty was that of a fresh model coming out of Vogue magazine.

"Line up kids" she would say in a very condescending manner. "Claire, Claire, help me line these kids up. We won't hit the piñata until everyone is properly in a single file line." It was always my job to take care of the kids. I was always in charge of them. Lydia would always tell parents "oh, yeah, Claire will watch your kids, she is so good with kids." She never asked me if I would like to help out, or if I had time to help out. She assumed I could do it and more often than not, she was right.

As soon as everyone lined up, she would make us be super quiet. She handed the smallest person the broomstick and would beckon me to go to the back of the line. I always felt pushed to the side. Being black, during that time period was no fun. Just like in the United States between the 20s' and 60s; the town I lived in had their own bouts of racism. The darker you were, the less use you were to the whites.

After everyone had their turn, and the piñata was almost on the ground, she would hand me the stick to "finish" the job. The bandana would get tied around my eyes and my adoptive father would twirl me around about five times. I was afraid that I would trip on a root and fall on my face.

He was tall. About 6'3 with reddish brown hair and green eyes. He weighed around 210 pounds and was our "Santa Claus" at every Christmas occasion. He was intelligent, a college graduate with two different doctorate degrees and he loved his job. He loved his job so much that he lived there. He was married to it.

"Ok, you ready Claire?" I could hear him say as he twirled me around. I was so dizzy that I would never respond. As the stick came down and met the piñata at the head, the candy came pouring out. That was all it took, one good smack and down it would go.
I wanted to experience the process, not the completion. But alas, that was my life.
Everyone would run to pick up candy before I was even done putting the broomstick down. By the time I was finished, the candy was gone. I had to fight off ants to get one little piece. As I opened up the wrapper, I flicked and brushed the ants off before they could bite. I was at war...me, against the ants...for that one piece of candy I wanted so badly; just to feel part of the celebration.

Parents came to pick up their kids, thank my APs for creating such an awesome party, and pull out of the driveway. After the party was well over, I would head back to the piñata area, just hoping that there would be a bit of candy around the roots.

Lydia was always watching to make sure I was not eating more than I "should."
"Claire, come in here and help us clean up the house. Your friends left such a mess here. Forget the candy, you don't need it anyway" she would shout from the window. She insisted on making my weight issue a PSA.

I would cock my head to one side, sad that I didn't get any candy from my own birthday party, shuffle my feet in the grass a bit in hopes that I would find a couple of left-behind pieces and then head back upstairs to clean.

Everyone gathered for dinner at around 7:00. We would talk about the day and how much we enjoyed it. I never expressed how I really felt about that day because I was afraid my a-mother would get mad at me. She always seemed mad at me and I never understood why.

A 4-8 hour Adoption Nightmare

July 6th 2015

I spent a lot of time in the past few weeks, watching 48-hour mystery episodes. I have especially been watching the "Live to Tell" series. It is really good but I find myself to be slightly unhealthily addicted to them…wink, sigh, chuckle…. eye-roll.

I am not sure if it is because I can relate to many of the stories, or if it is because I have a bit of "sociopath" in me (according to those little quizzes on Facebook). Whatever the reason, watching these episodes have brought me back to difficult situations in my life that I felt would have been different if I were the white blue-eyed, blonde, tall, skinny legged, daughter my a-mother adored so much.

I never felt like I fit in. It is a feeling that I can never put into words. Being an "Oreo," like my red-headed WAF would always say, made me feel so small, like I did not belong to any side. They used to laugh at me for not being able to "dance like a black person" or "speak like a black person." They used to criticize me for not knowing how to speak my mother tongue.

My a-mother in particular would get real upset when I wanted to learn how to speak the Spanish language (once we moved to the neighboring Latino country from Haiti), because she believed that only English was important and Spanish was not necessary. When I picked up the language within 3 weeks of moving there, she was real jealous that I was able to comprehend the locals. She on the other hand, had spent years in Latin American countries and still could not speak the language. I think that was the control freak in her; Lydia wanted to control everything from what I ate to how I dressed, to how much water I could drink.

It was overwhelming to say the least.

But the breaking point came when I was around 17 years old. I remember it like it was yesterday. My a-mother had forced me to exercise. As a 17-year-old, being forced to do anything was annoying. I was asserting my independence but for some reason, this time, I felt I had to do it. It was the last walk I would take for years, especially down that scary path.

My a-father was quiet, and quite the opposite of outspoken. As a matter of fact, he didn't have a voice at all. Except for that horrible night. I saw him in a very different light. He stayed behind. He didn't leave out the back door with the others…. he stayed with me, the black adopted child….and endured horrific pain.

The home invasion didn't start immediately. I got my jogging shoes on and started down the path. It was still early so I could time it properly. I'd be back just before the sun went down. I arrived at the gate (a 15-minute walk downhill) and turned around. While walking back up, I felt that something was a bit off. I had no idea…I was tired, my legs hurt and I was fucking pissed off at Lydia for forcing me to do physical exercise and my other siblings didn't have to. She never forced the white children to do anything. They were perfect…and I felt, well, like I was nothing.

I climbed the paved road that led to the top of the small mountain. Only a few more minutes and then I would be up at the big house, I'd be able to go and shower, and I'd be able to prepare for a dinner that I would not be allowed to fully enjoy because it would be controlled by my a-mother. She never let me serve myself. She thought that my stomach was the size of her stomach (the size of a fist) because she had many eating issues that she would never admit to. She believed that being skinny was the way to go. Her obsession with the physical appearance was out of this world. So when she served my plate, everything was measured so that I didn't "overeat." All the while my siblings ate chicken legs, chicken breast, tons of potatoes, heaps of rice…all the good stuff my body craved…. but nope, I was not allowed to have it. I was allowed a slice of bread, a piece of chicken and a few vegetables….and at times, even that was too much…the funny thing was…. I was already a practicing anorexic and Lydia thought that since it made me thinner, it was beautiful.

As I approached the top of the hill, I saw 3-4 men wearing some kind of facial covering. They grabbed me and pushed me to the ground. All I could do was pray, pray so fervently that this would be over real soon. But it was not. About 8 hours into the ordeal, my a-mother had "slipped out the door" with the other kids….my a-father had stayed behind and did what a parent is supposed to do; to protect their child. What happened between hour 1 and hour 8 was nothing short of horrific. The home invasion was in full swing and my life was on the line. I wrote about this in my book called *Jogging to Hell*. Suffice it to say I was brutalized and forever traumatized.

But I lived to tell. I lived to tell about it and I am not sure why. I wish they had taken my life then and there. I was not happy growing up in a white home, I was not happy with who I was as a person. After the home invasion and being held hostage, I grew even more bitter and angry with Lydia.

Why did she leave me?

Why didn't she stay behind?

Would everyone have died?

Did she do the right thing?

Was I less important to her?

Did she think I was strong enough to go through the humiliation and violation I had suffered at the hands of those men?

Was God really that evil?

Was I not worth it?

I had so many more questions about my place in the family after that horrific night. I bonded with my a-father throughout the entire ordeal. I watched my physically disabled brother be left behind as well.

Was he not worth being saved either?

Later, after being fully negatively affected by the horrible torment, Lydia told me that when they arrived to town by foot (through the forest), they summoned the police. I didn't want the police. At 17 years of age, I wanted her near me, hugging me, being there for me.

I wanted her to stay behind with me....

to sacrifice herself for me ...

at that point, I wanted her to *save* me.

That is what I would have done for my daughter, I would not have fled with the others. Never...ever...ever!

As I watch these Live to Tell episodes, I think to myself how I was able to "live to tell" my story. But living to tell often leaves more pain, guilt, and hurt. I didn't want to live to tell. I didn't want those horrible memories of Jake (my a-father) being incapacitated. I didn't want to relive the gunshots that left me partially deaf in one ear.

I didn't want to see any more blood in my dreams,

I didn't want to see more cuts on his back.

I didn't want to smell the men's breath as they breathed over me...

I didn't want to remember what they smelled like,

tasted like,

felt like.

I didn't want to remember how much I HATED God....and Jesus, And the Angels.... I didn't want to be ME.

I didn't want to think that....
I...WAS...NOT...WORTH....IT.

If only I had not been adopted, and if only I fit in, would I be the one to run away with Lydia and my siblings?

If it were Nora being held hostage, would she have stayed for her?

So many questions are left unanswered in my heart and mind. All I can think of is not repeating the same mistakes....and never hoping or wishing this on anyone. But with this separation I currently have with my a-mother, I wonder what her side of the story is.

Who was I to her?

Who am I to her?

Am I the daughter who was the triangle in the circular peg?

Am I just the girl who wrote a book and told her story?

Am I the adopted child who Lived to Tell?

Yes.... yes, I AM.

Adopted but not Equal

November 1st 2015

Did you know that Haiti threatened to not stamp my passport because they could not understand why I had a Haitian passport? They believed I should have a US passport and according to their records, being adopted by US a-parents meant I was a US citizen.

"Where is your US passport?" they would ask me in Creole/French. It is hard to explain everything I feel and how much I don't understand the answer to their question. There was no time to explain. I just needed my passport stamped so that I could proceed with my daughter's legal adoption.

I'm not looking for pity; I'm looking for change.

Ever since I can remember, I've lived with an American family. Both of my a-parents are American Citizens and I was adopted from an orphanage in Haiti.

With adoption, comes the responsibilities that follow; physical, spiritual, physiological and emotional care are all part of what keeps a person alive. But what allows a person to be successful, and able to pursue life, liberty and happiness, is making sure they have the same rights you have.

My US citizen APs did not get US citizenship for me and thus I've had to navigate on a visitor's visa all my life. I'm blessed to be able to have a visa and many people would give up materialistic things to be able to have that important stamp in their passport.

I am also extremely blessed to have been given the kind of life that affords me certain luxuries that may not have been available to me had I not been united in this fashion. I am thankful to the force that keeps everything moving forward for me and my family.

I am just thankful in general!

But I believe I should not be one of those "lucky" people who got the stamp. I should be one of those people who has the opportunity to work for the US government; approving the stamps for those who qualify, apply, qualify, and want to see more of the world. I want to be the consular official on the other side of the desk saying "you are approved!" In order to do this, I need that US passport. I should have received citizenship as a legally adopted child of US citizens.

Many of you reading may not know what it is like to stand for many hours waiting to be approved to enter a country you should have citizenship for. Many reading, have not experienced denial of a visa to a country you wish to explore. Some of you reading will not ever feel your stomach churning, your heart racing, and then tears filling your eyes when hearing "denied" for the 4th, 5th and even 6th time. I'm fortunate that I have never been denied a US visa. But I've been denied visas to different parts of the world due to me not having a US passport. I've been denied visas to countries my adoptive family have traveled to for Christmas and thus; left behind. I've been required to get a visa for the country I resided in for over 20 years.

And many of you may know how it feels to experience all of the above. Even more of a reason to extend a helping hand to those who are placed incorrectly into the system.

It has not been easy, and many times I was considered "inadmissible" because of the passport I hold. I missed a-family gatherings, and have been questioned numerous times as to why I was not a US citizen. I could never answer the "why."

I've been blessed though because even though I have been denied entry into many places, having a US visa allows me to be granted visas to other places. But that too comes with a cost. I have traveled to different parts of the world. But as a foreigner, I must use visahq.com, my trusted site, to let me know where I need a visa and how much it costs. visa requirements for Haitian citizens can be found on Wikipedia and other helpful sites. If you visit the website, you will notice that Haitians can travel visa- free or visa-on-arrival to 40-45 countries. Some countries allow for travel if the Haitian passport has a EU, Canadian, or US visa. Some countries require prior authorization in order to travel. According to the passport index this ranks Haiti as the 77th passport in the World. This does not sound good. The UK and the US passports are ranked at # 1. To view your passport ranking visit the passport index. Many of these countries that admit Haitians require a stop in the US. So without a US visa, traveling to these other countries is nearly impossible.

I don't know the "why" to the question, I just know that for some reason, the US did not consider me one of them. Was it an oversight of the US government? Was it lack of interest of my US adoptive parents? I won't ever know. But

I believe a combination of the two equals a case such as this one.

And It is not just me.

This indeed is my personal story and I know I am not alone.
There are children adopted by US citizens, and living in the US who are subject to deportation at this very moment. They are being treated like aliens in a country they were raised in. This is not fair and I want to see this treatment end; not just for me but for everyone involved.

Without US citizenship we don't have equal rights:

1. We are unable to work without special authorization.
2. We are unable to open our own business unless we employ US citizens or have a Green Card.
3. We are unable to attend school without authorization and/or a special visa or Green Card.
4. Traveling to different countries is brutally difficult and many times we are asked to pay extra for visas ahead of time and even oftentimes denied. Having a Green Card helps.
5. We are unable to easily get medical care or health insurance.
6. We are unable to vote.
7. Our social security card says "not valid for employment" unless we have a Green Card.
8. We are never seen as belonging to the US or any of its territories, when we should.
9. We are always under suspicion.
10. We are aliens.
11. We may pass on the same legacy to our children.

There are more restrictions to not having a US passport but I just listed a few.

There is currently a Bill in congress (S.2275)* asking to **grant equality to foreign adopted children whose adoptive parents failed to acquire U.S. citizenship before they turned 18.**

It would be great to have more and more people sign this petition and help financially. The reference page will give you more information.

You can also read stories about other children/adults who have suffered the consequences of their a-parents not fulfilling their duties and the government failing to grant equality.

I believe something needs to be done. If the government can't right this wrong, I think they should at least help with the expenses associated with "starting over." If there is not a fast track to solving this problem, I think a law must be put into place stating that American Citizens *cannot* adopt children overseas unless they plan to completely fulfill their commitment and obligation to their foreign adopted children.

There must be requirements in order to make sure the foreign born child becomes a citizen. PLEASE comply with the requirements, even if it makes you uncomfortable. You may be asked to move to the US for a short period of time (for those living internationally). PLEASE do so to establish residency for your child.

Regardless of fault (US government, or US a-parents), the wrong needs to be righted. And I will stop at nothing to make sure justice prevails!

So let me tell you about the fees for starting over. Everything is so expensive and when you have dependents, prepare to pay more. There are certain forms that are required as adult adoptees "starting over."

Here is a general breakdown in US dollars for adoptees (and their kids) who are having to start the process over. I am using my family as an example.

1. I-130: Petition for Alien Relative (each relative)-420 x # of applicants.

2. G-325a: Biography (each person files)-0 but if filing from the US, which we are. There is a fee if filing outside the US.

3. I-864: Affidavit of Support (person who can guarantee finances support)-0 but if filing from the US. There is a fee if filing outside the US.

4. I-693: Medical-fees vary by civil surgeon-(around 400.00 per person).

5. I-485: adjustment of Status-1,070.00 (includes biometrics).

6. I-765: Work Authorization -465.00 (free if filed with adjustment of status).

7. I-131: advanced parole, or permission to leave the US and return (each person in family should file)-805.00 if filed separately from the original petition.

Make sure to file it together so as not to be charged extra.

And then there are lawyer/attorney Fees.
8. Attorney fees ranges from 2200-3900 dollars.

Adoptive parents, naturalize your children immediately so that they don't need to go through all of this when they are older. Your children are family, and should be treated equally-just like biological children.

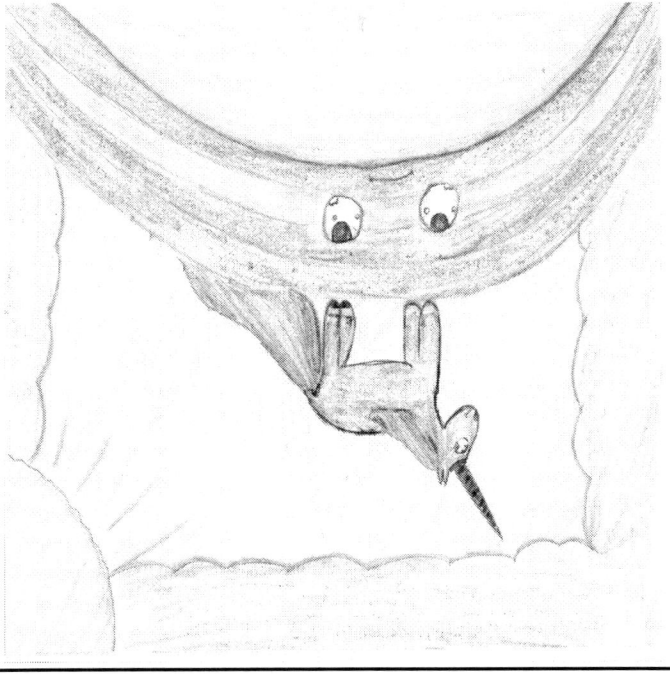

LOSS

Is My Haitian Child Haitian?

April 7ᵗʰ 2015

"Why are they holding my passport?" I asked the kind Haitian man to my right. I was so lucky he spoke enough English, and that I was able to have a conversation with him.

"They are saying you are not Haitian," He told me as they returned my passport, un-stamped. The passport did not get stamped which would mean I would not legally be allowed to enter into Haiti; my birth country.

I was on my 3rd trip into Haiti. My foster daughter, of whom I have complete legal guardianship of, lives with me in the Dominican. We started the process in 2012.

The fact that I could not understand what the Haitian people were saying during border check was depressing and upsetting at the same time. I AM HAITIAN but alas, was not raised in this fashion.

A little after birth, I was transferred to an orphanage, where I proceeded to spend the next 3-4 years. When I turned around four years old, I was adopted by Whites.

A curse and a blessing at the same time is how I actually see it. Blessed to have a home, but cursed to never really be able to call myself "Haitian." The little Creole I know, I learned from the handy man who lived with my a-family doing odd jobs. But it was minimal.

They never completed the adoption (in the US) so I still had a Haitian passport. This passport is one of the least desired forms of identification in the world because of its limitations. Why they chose not to complete the adoption process is beyond me. That is another story.
The story I am telling is that of me being Haitian by passport but white in every other sense.

DON'T TURN YOUR Haitian/Black ADOPTED CHILD INTO A white HUMAN BEING.

This specific story is aimed at people who adopt Haitian kids, but it really is a global issue.

Do not adopt unless you are ready to fully embrace their culture.

Some questions need to be asked by you and your family BEFORE you adopt.

1. Why am I adopting?

2. Who am I adopting?

3. What do I hope will occur once I adopt?

4. What are my plans for family blending?

5. How do I keep my Haitian Child's Heritage and traditions alive?

6. Can I help them maintain their Creole (for kids 5+) or can I teach them Creole (for babies+).

<u>White in a Haitian Body</u>

April 10th 2015

As he handed me back the passport, un-stamped, my body and mind went through total cognitive dissonance. "I have to prove to him that I am Haitian," I thought to myself as tears slowly rolled down my cheeks.

Living on the other side of the island for over 20 years did not help the fact that my Creole was now a third language to be learned. The little Creole I learned, I acquired from the handyman who worked at my house as a child.

I learned Spanish fluently, and since the other side of the island is Spanish, I was surrounded by it and therefore, did not lose it.

Haitian Creole on the other hand was a completely different story.

I remember sitting in a truck when I was around 4 years old. I bumped up and down as the dirt road winded over the hills and mountains as I approached my new home in Haiti-the home away from the only home I knew; the orphanage. I could only speak Creole then. I had no English, no Spanish…just utterances of Creole.

I was about four years old but yet, walking had yet to be part of my everyday life. Later, after going back and researching my orphanage and speaking with people who cared for me, and knew of me, I was told that there was a handful of children who rarely saw the light of day. They were stuffed into a small dark room with no more than 1 meal per day, and no place to use the bathroom. I was part of that handful. And this is why the "normal" growth process did not apply to me-or none of the other abandoned children in the small dark room.

"If I don't speak to the officer at the counter, he won't let me into Haiti, and I NEED to be there. My lawyer is waiting for me," I said to the man who accompanied me back to the counter after being denied entrance once.

"Mwe pa pale Creole anpil pase que mwe te crie lote bwa." That is what I could muster up. My Creole was nowhere near good or satisfactory, but that seemed to be enough to let me in. I was hoping......

I asked my readers to answer the following questions to get an idea of where they are on the adoption journey. I went ahead and answered the questions too...because I too am in the process of adoption.

1. Why am I adopting? I want to be able to travel with my daughter. She has been living with me for the past 8 years and though I have legal guardianship of her, it is not enough in the eyes of US law to travel. So adopting opens the world to her and it also strips her of her identity. This is something that I will need to be open to talking about as she gets older.

2. Who am I adopting? My daughter came to me at the age of 4. Her mother was desperate and left two children at my door step. I cared for the two kids for about 4 months when I realized that I no longer had the funds to raise both of them. At the same time, I was fostering two more children. The youngest one returned to her biological mother but the older one refused to go. She had a strong temperament. In that instance I had to make a lifelong and life-changing decision. If the older one was to stay with me, it would be a forever thing, there is no "going" back. She is young enough for me to make a huge impression on her life. I told her several times that she needed to go back to her mother. She cried and cried and cried, knowing that she would go home to no electricity, a one room house (everything in one room) and dirty drinking water. She told me she did not want to go. I gave her a few days to think it over. Yes, at 4 you wouldn't think that decisions like that can be made by a child but she surprised me. 8 years later, she is now 12 and is not the same person I took in at 4. I am adopting a 12-year-old Haitian girl. She did not choose to be adopted, she chose to have electricity and a house to live in. She chose to feel safe.

3. What do I hope will occur once I adopt? Once I adopt I will be carrying about our daily routine. Since she has already been with me, I am not really waiting for her to "come home to me," I am just waiting to be able to show her more of the world.

4. What are my plans for family blending? For us, family blending happened the minute she was dropped off at my house with her little sister. I had two older children, a seven-year-old and a twelve-year-old. I had been raising both these children since real young and my daughter was entering into a new world with a lot of new wonders. She spoke the Spanish language as did my other two children so adjusting culture/language-wise was not hard. Learning to speak English came three years later. She listened for the first three years and then one day, just opened her mouth and started speaking. If you were to speak with her today, you would think she was African American. Adjusting was a bit simpler but there still were many issues-bed wetting, going to the bathroom in places other than the toilet, hitting, scratching., crying, hiding food, sneaking food. Eating so much that she would throw up minutes later. It took some times to work with her on these issues. Once she realized that there would ALWAYS be enough food, those issues began to clear up. She was also fascinated with electricity. The blending component was a bit of a struggle because my two older daughters had Latino long flowing hair while she had spongy 4c hair. She was often jealous of her sister's hair.

5. How do I keep my Haitian Child's Heritage and traditions alive? To be honest, this is the toughest question I will probably ever have to answer. Being Haitian myself, it is quite embarrassing to think that I was not able to pass down my own heritage to my Haitian kids. Then, I realized that it is not about fault. It is about what to do from here on out. So I got to thinking. I hired a Haitian woman (several years ago) to watch my kids while I was at work, and once they got home from School. That way they would hear Haitian Creole. The issue here was that living on the other side of the island, everyone speaks Spanish. So, even that plan didn't work out too well. Then as my daughter got older, I offered to pay the lady I hired more money if she would ONLY speak Haitian Creole to her. That didn't work either because by then (child was about 8) she had already lost all her Creole. As a black Haitian (raised by Americans), I did not speak Creole to my children because I myself was not confident enough. I try to keep the heritage alive by reminding her who she is, how beautiful it is to be black and Haitian. I also get super excited when she has culture events at school and we get to go all "Haitian" on her classmates. I'm not quite sure what that even entails. You have to understand the history of Haiti and its neighbor to fully understand why Haitian kids deny their heritage, adopted or not. I didn't want that to start to happen to my daughter but believe it or not, it did begin to happen….and it was scary. It took me back to when I was 8 years old.

6. Can I help them maintain their Creole (for kids 5+) or can I teach them Creole (for babies+) Helping my daughter keep Creole will be hard but I have made steps towards it. For us, we both study French. We use Duolingo.com and she does two lessons a week on the weekends and when she is on holiday, she does a lesson a day. She enjoys it but because she is not hearing it spoken, she is not really picking it up as much as I would like her to. Soon we will move to the center of the country and I am hoping that I can enroll her in a French/Creole public school where she will be surrounded by children of her color, nationality and birth language.

Chandelier and a Stolen Passport

April 16ᵗʰ 2015

I was determined to learn the song Chandelier by Sia. My daughter knows practically every song on Spotify and Pandora but I have limited her options to only Pandora since I can monitor and use parental controls. But there is something about Sia's song that made me want to learn it. Maybe it was the high notes that she sings in the chorus and seems to carry on till the awkward bridge, or maybe it is just what the song is about.

As I was learning the song (because a complicated song takes time and you have to break it up into small sections and repeat those sections over and over again) I noticed that her addiction to alcohol is like my addiction to finding out when my daughter's adoption will be final. I've been hanging on for so long and just doing things to occupy myself (along with crying).

It is essential that while you are waiting (if the kids are with you), you live your life as if this is where you are going to be for the rest of it. I broke down a few days ago and after hearing that my passport won't be ready for "six" months, and the adoption is not final, that I am pretty doomed. At times I feel that everything I set out to do has not positively come to fruition.

The other little detail I noticed about Sia's song is that I so desperately want and need to learn the Creole language. So as I was breaking apart Sia's interesting song, and actually learned the entire thing.... I realized that it truly is possible.... anything, within reason, is possible.

I left you guys in the last chapter hearing about my desperate attempt to prove to the officials that I, despite my lack of an English accent, and American body language, and education, and intelligence, and may I add, beauty (all things that Haitians generally are not used to hearing or being a part of-from the mindset of its neighbor), I truly am Haitian. I had to come up with something that would prove it. It was not enough to have my adoption papers, my birth certificate and my passport all with me. It was not enough to be black, with the sponge-bob-square pants hair in every crevice of my body. It was not enough to have a booklet branded with the symbols of Haiti's accomplishments and lack thereof, it was not enough to be able to speak a few words. In the eyes of the Haitian immigration people at the border, I had…. yes…. I had stolen this Haitian passport and applied a German last name to the end of my "actual" name.

I kid you not…you can't make up a story like this…. I was under speculation because my last name was NOT Haitian, oh no it was not. It also was not American, nor Canadian. It was indeed German and it means Royal Armorer. So how does a so-called Haitian obtain a Haitian passport, but has a German last name?

Well, she must have stolen it.

The man helping me through this whole ordeal looked at me with a super serious face (most Haitians are confused with being completely angry and about to attack because our faces show our present feelings…. there is no pretending in Haiti) and asked me if I had stolen the passport. At this point, my eyes began to tear up…. again. "No, I did not steal this passport…I was never given a US passport. My APs are American but neglected to take the right steps to make sure I was in "good" hands. Their mission work took precedence over my protection."

"Well mam," (yes, he called me mam….so polite of him). "The officers believe that this is not your passport." At this point I angrily cursed my adoptive parents…. I was so upset with them, after years and years of struggle, not being able to travel as much as I would have liked to, being questioned at every border when wanting to visit a friend and being forever labeled as a member of "that country" I vowed that my daughter WOULD NOT go through what I have gone through…yes, ALL of my life.

"You can't get in" the officer told my friend. "Mwe pa kapab entre?" I repeated in my limited Creole. He raised his eyebrows and said……

Happy Place and Custom Forms

January 20th 2016

According to my adoptive mother, we were not "that" type of Christian. I never really knew what *that* type of Christian really was, I just knew that I didn't want to be that in the future.

Anyone who was not like us was way too fundamental. I remember my a-mother smiling her fake smile as we registered one more religious group. I was in charge of making sure the dorms were prepped with proper bedding and the toiletries in the bathroom were sufficient. Then I would have to go upstairs and set the table. Plates facing downward as to keep them clean for the big supper that was to be inhaled.

I loved the groups really. It was my way of being part of "real" life. The people from the south were always the best company because of their ability to sing and hold great harmony, and their accents were unforgettable. I looked forward to new people each week because I was a student at heart-and in real life. I loved to learn, to sing new songs, and get to know new people. I would eventually get their email addresses or physical addresses and then later spend hours writing letters to them. They were my connection to the outside world. I wanted so much to be out of the world I was in. I wanted to be able to converse like them, understand their jokes better, pray and sing like them. I was naive in my own way because I was kept in this little bubble and my a-mother had no desire for anyone to pop it. She liked the control she had over her husband, boyfriend and kids. She lived each day for that control.

We were very sheltered, my siblings and I were. Though today, if I were to speak with any of them, they would side with my a-mother. We were very *Christian* if I can use that term. But as I said before, we were not *that* kind of Christian. We were better than *that* kind of Christian.

As my a-mother showed her fake smile, she logged her groups into the really old ThinkPad computer we had sitting in the kitchen (this was back in 2000). The kitchen was massive and it was on the second floor. This was the second kitchen on the compound.

You see, we were rich.... not rich in spirit I feel, rich in possessions, things, buildings, houses, property, dogs, money, cars.... people who trusted us. Not me necessarily, but them-the ones orchestrating the fake love just to get some money to "build homes." Don't get me wrong, they did build homes with most of the money, but it was the rest of the money that I always questioned.

But I was not allowed to know.

I couldn't ask her any questions as a child and even less did I ask her as an adult. The biggest question however is "Why didn't you complete the adoption and give me US citizenship?" But to this day, I am afraid I would get the fake answer; the answer that only begged me to ask more questions.

She was always afraid that people would find out the truth, so she hid it.... under the same rug we walked on each and every day. Sometimes I would lay on that rug and cry myself to sleep, hoping and praying for a new group to come so that I could return to my "happy place" of being part of something bigger and a bit more exciting.

I spent so many days and nights hearing the words "no, no, no" that it didn't surprise me to hear the officer at the border say "No, you can't get in." "Mwe pa kapab entre?" I repeated in my limited Creole. The officer raised his eyebrows and said "ah, me ou pale Creole." I smiled wide and I'm sure the dimple that I had always had was being seen even bigger and brighter than before.

I told him that my Creole was not good but that there are plenty of Haitians who live in the United States and around the world who don't speak a lick of Creole. I then asked him "li pa haitien?" He nodded as if to tell me that he got it. My new friend who rode the bus with me stood by my side and smiled.

He took my passport back and compared my customs form with my passport. He told me that the writing order was not the same. I showed him, as fear welled up in my voice, that it was the same that I had just written my middle name before my last name (which is normal to do) but apparently it was not the same on my passport. He gave me a new application to fill out and I filled it out at the back table. Thankfully I had a working pen in my purse because all of those attached black pens never worked-the ink was either too light or completely nonfunctional.

As I filled out the form, I felt my hand shake from frustration. I was not sure why I was being told to fill out this nasty long-ass form for the second time.

Finally, I was done and took my passport and form back up to the counter. The officer at the counter looked at it and said "ou fe li mal ankoa." Indeed, I had filled it out exactly how I had done earlier. He shook his head and……

Sometimes I just want to be Sexy

April 29th 2015

After taking back the passport and customs form, and redoing the assignment (I felt like I was in elementary school, being graded for an assignment done poorly), I handed it back to the official dude at the counter. With little to no smile, he took the items from me, put them up to the light and placed it back on the table.

"Now what?" I asked him in poor, choppy, disguised Creole "sac pasee?"

"Ayien" he said and then looked at the other officer standing beside him. He showed the officer my passport. Both took turns pointing at me, and then looking back at the picture. They were both giggling. Something must have been terribly funny.

Then, they called over a police guard clear across the waiting room. The police guard waded through the crowd. I started to feel a bit nervous. Not only are they giggling when they look at my passport, but they are also beckoning a police person to come "see this."

The guard did not even have the decency to say excuse me. As he came across the way, he looked at what the officer was showing everyone else. They were looking at my passport picture.

Taking a passport pictures is a very serious thing. In Haiti and many other Latin American countries, one is not encouraged to smile, wear any accessories is prohibited, and one does not even hint at being "happy." So my passport picture was befitting. I looked ugly. This was just one more elaborate way to keep me out of my birth country. Maybe if they laughed loud enough, I would turn around and leave.

I looked like a tall, slightly overweight, short-haired African male. And to top it off, I had a slight squint which was a lot more apparent since one is not allowed to wear glasses when taking passport photos. So I did not feel pretty at all.

I felt hideous.

So as everyone around the officer was looking at my photo, giggling at me, laughing at the photo, looking back at me, I just felt this overwhelming desire to throw up. I felt that I was actually being visually molested. I was helpless. If I grabbed the passport, would they remember me and not let me in the next time? Would they arrest me?

Would they not stamp my damn passport????

Haiti is not a lawless country, it is a country where people don't know how, nor choose, to follow the law. So one never knows when they will spend a few hours in a jail cell. So I really had to choose my battles.

My friend who was with me asked to have the passport. They kindly gave it to him and yelled during the transaction "ce'st un monsier."

When I was a baby, I was extremely mal-nourished. When I eventually was put into an orphanage, food nor care was enough to keep me from getting a squint. I was also locked in a closet for days at a time which I am sure did not help with my health. By the time I got to my adoptive parents (4 years later), my eyesight had already been cut by a large percentage and one eye decided that it would make decisions for itself.

Sometimes I just want to be sexy. It is hard to feel wanted or even sexy when you live with a disability that you really can't change it.

So it is something I live with on a daily basis. Things could of course be worse. I am healthy now, and loved by my partner but it is sometimes hard to feel "sexy" in an unsexy body. And in this country, and in Haiti, beauty is even more subjective because these countries are so male dominated.

My passport was stamped eventually but now the issues were about to get that much worse.......

The Green light and Jealousy

May 8th 2015

Finally, after a good 40 minutes that felt like an hour, I was given the green light to actually enter my birth country.

The Haitian officials were happily making fun of my passport picture and all I wanted was to feel "sexy." The moment I realized they were making fun of me, a deep sense of sadness settled in my soul. The standards of beauty in Haiti was skewed. They only focused on the physical. I soon realized however, that they were the ones who were unhappy.

In such a poor country, officials who do government work are not respected to the full. They are underpaid and often times don't even get fed on any given day.

They too are fending for themselves.

I realized that people laugh at others because they see something they are lacking. They feel jealous and even envious. They will never admit it, but they are hurting inside.

As the officials looked at my passport that was riddled with visas from many different countries, they felt a sense of loss. The furthest they probably have gone was to the Dominican, and even then, treated like nothing.

If I knew Creole, I am sure my confidence would have been much, much higher. I would have been able to communicate with them, crack a joke or two, sit down for a coffee…but alas, my a-parents stripped me of that part of my identity.

The Dominican and Haiti have a long standing bad history of racism. It continues today as I watch lighter kids throw rocks and make fun of semi darker kids. I see it when I get into public transport and I am asked to sit at the "back of the bus." Yes, I said it. Just like during the Montgomery Boycott Era.

Rosa Parks is truly one of my heroes. Here, in the Dominican, Haitians are still treated as 3rd class citizens, because they treat dogs better than Haitians.

I am fortunate my daughter did not suffer the way I have in the past. I am stronger because of it though. I have written a bit about my suffering in my first book called *A Failed Adoption: Who is your Larimar?*

I would be lying if I said I am not mad at my a-family for the way they treated me as a child and for their unreasonable expectations. I am hurt more than anything. Anger does not even begin to describe the pain one goes through. Anger keeps me from being able to move forward though.

But I feel an overwhelming sense of loss.

I can't say whether it was done on purpose or not, but I can say that many years of observation has led to the knowledge that they could have made it happen but they chose not to. In some ways my a-mother wanted me to be a white American, resembling her biological kids in stature and intelligence. But on the other hand, when groups came to do mission work, she wanted me to be black as night in order to gloat over what "she has done" in God's name and how she has been the *savior.*

So I lived my life thinking that I was white both inside and out. If you were to hear me speak, and not see my face, you would think I was a white woman from the Midwest.

God and I are pretty close. No, I am not a "Christian" in the former sense of the word. But I do love God and trust God's power and hand in everything I do. I have learned to forgive because forgiveness is not for the other person but for myself. Without forgiveness, I would not be where I am today.

As I got back on the bus to enter Haiti, I took a deep breath. I knew that I would not be intimidated the way I was at the border. My lawyer, though odd, is kind and is understanding toward my situation. He is not impressed with the fact that I don't speak Creole, but he does "get it." He thinks my English is through the roof and says he wishes he could speak like me.

What can we take away from this?

If you have adopted internationally, please, please, please, see that your child does not lose their birth language, the one that was spoken to them while they were in the womb.

Their mother tongue is so important.

There are many ways to help your child maintain their birth language. The key is to start right away.

1. Tell them who they are from the get-go.

2. Explain to them who their parents are (if you know who they are).

3. Be open with them about their adoption.

4. Tell them what race they are. (this may be super controversial but it is important they don't think they are white-if you are white).

5. DO NOT change their name. (My first, middle and last name was changed).

6. At night, read to them in Creole (or birth language).

7. Let them listen to Haitian or their culture's music in the bathtub.

8. When they are of writing age, sign them up for birth language lessons online or at a center near you. My daughter uses babel.com, and Alison.com and duolingo.com.

9. DO NOT try and change their appearance. If they insist, walk them through it and explain, in a positive manner, the outcome.

10. If there are other Haitian (matching races) kids in the neighborhood, create a co-op that celebrates and unites children of all backgrounds and encourage your child to participate.

11. Encourage the WHOLE family to participate in the language learning process. Soon your child will be the leader. Let him/her teach!

12. Let them be who they are!

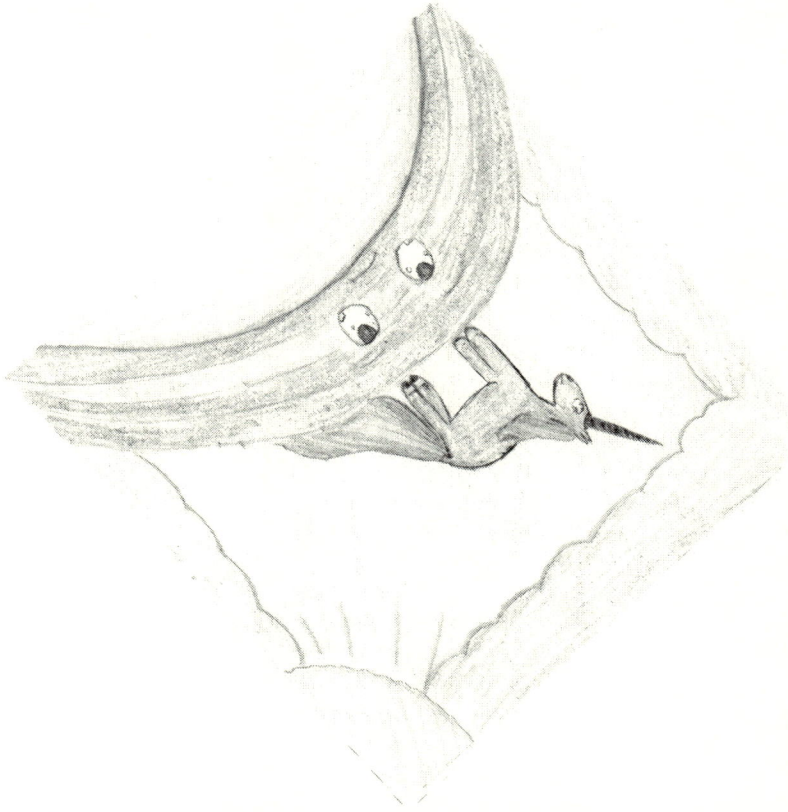

AWARENESS

Her belief

My sister and I were very close when we were younger. We both believed in something that helped us get through each day. For her, it was unicorns. There was something about unicorns that made her feel safe. She collected *EVERYTHING* unicorn and she got really upset when she found out that unicorns actually did not exist. Instead of believing in this new found truth, she decided to attach a cone onto a rhinoceros, imitating a unicorn.

It made her feel better.

It made her feel like life was peachy fuzz.

I remember asking my sister one day what made her believe in unicorns and she said it was because her life was so amazing and therefore, unicorns had to exist.

Unfortunately, it was not the case for me. I didn't believe in unicorns. I believed strongly in the aids virus that killed so many people. I believed in constant pain. I believed in wet sheets in the morning. I believed in hurt feelings on a daily basis; on life under insurmountable stress, in an existence that would not stop existing. I could not believe in anything else. My life as I saw it was not about it being "wonderful," it was about it being horrible, sad, and filled with daily and nightly tears.

I was adopted at a real young age; black child adopted into a white family who did not know how to raise a child of color. I was adopted into a family who thought that body weight should be the same, clothing should be worn in the same way, tummies should be filled (or not filled) based on the hunger index of a narcissistic woman who called herself my "mother." I was raised with an a-father whose sarcasm was drowning in racism not toward for my skin hue, but toward that of anyone who was not like him. I was raised with a man who called himself my "uncle" but had no blood relation, nor affiliation to any of my parents except for the purpose of sleeping with my mother. And feigning to be an authority figure. I was surrounded by three other children of color who didn't see themselves as children of color. They saw themselves as white; because our role models were just that.

White.

I was raised in a country where my color was not welcomed, even though those around me matched my color to a T. But it was not just my color that was not wanted, it was my race. I am African, with Haitian parents who loved me to the point of wanting to give me a better life (this is what my adoptive parents told me).

For me, I could not believe in unicorns because I did not see my life the way my sister saw it. I did not have joy; I did not have peace. Every night I went to bed, I hoped to not wake up again. I thought I had aids because I had been violated on numerous occasions-leaving me helpless and wanting to return to the dust from which I came.

You see, when my sister was told that unicorns were not real, she created her own unicorn; a fantasy that would fit her idea and worldview. I wish I could create a fantasy that would catapult me into another world where I do not have to deal with having to tell my a-parents about the abuse I endured at their own hands, and the hands of those they "trusted." I wanted to be the one riding a unicorn.

I wanted to be the one who could gallop away, far into the distance, never looking back.

I wanted to be the one to believe that things were amazing.

So I started to pretend, only to find out later that I was the rainbow the unicorn walked on. I was the child who made people feel amazing, and great and wonderful and beautiful. But I was also the child people walked on, trampled over, and mistook for "just some colors the light is reflecting."

Unicorns do not exist. They are created. If we allow our belief in adoption to skew the reality that is the life we face today, we will create children who believe in things that do not exist, who believe in things that make them think that life is a fantasy. We ourselves will begin to believe things about adoption that are just not true. We will make our adopted children into rainbows, forcing them to smile, and be happy, and radiate light, color, and beauty, while trampling on their very soul. We will be the false image of reality.

We will become the unicorn, even if it is just the cone on a rhinoceros.

Sex Toy

I was around 6 years old when I first heard someone yell out their window in Spanish "GIVE ME YOUR PUSSY". I had no idea what a pussy was nor did I really think they were talking to me. But as I continued to walk down the road on my own (headed to my favorite mango tree), I heard them say it again. What was a pussy? And why were they telling me to give it to them?

I was 12 years old when I was assaulted for not "meeting the sexual expectations." I was walking with my a-father to pick up dinner and someone threw two oranges at my head. They were half eaten and one hit the ground. I was clearly upset and my a-father did nothing to help me. He was as shocked as I was and still said nothing. On the drive home there was complete silence.

He didn't know what to say, and I chose not to relive the horror of me being an object to him, so I kept my mouth shut.

In the Dominican, we are taught real young that our bodies do not belong to us. Our bodies belong to men, big, evil, and mean men.

In 2015 I left an area in the Dominican for good. My daughter, wife and I packed up our belongings and decided that we would no longer make our presence known in Sosna (my childhood home). Never to return there, as sex was written on the walls of every corner and the sky had drawn it up on its clouds. The area we lived in was frequently visited by male suitors from the US, Canada and different parts of Europe. Black children and little black girls were expected to dance for the men and then sexually perform with them.

To them, we were sex toys.

We didn't even know what sex was, but yet we were their toys.

When we first moved to Sosna, I was so little and naïve. We went from living in the country-side to living closer to town, in a new neighborhood, and in a completely new country.

Sex was for sale and the younger you were, the more expensive. We moved to a place where my pussy, your pussy, and his penis was what the men from out of the country wanted. So the assumption was that if you were a white foreigner, you were also doing it. You were buying sex, you were having sex at all hours of the day and night, and you were even selling sex. It was believed that you were having sex with your family members.

My adoptive father, as you may recall, is white. And I, as you may recall, am black. So we had a huge issue. I learned to hate going out in public with him because I learned almost immediately that he was expected to parade me around, as if I was his sex prize.

I was supposed to be his sex toy.

He would never have done any of these things I mentioned but imagine living in fear and having this constant ill feeling in the pit of your stomach.... the kind that makes you want to throw up. The kind that makes you pee all over yourself in your sleep, the kind that makes you become a recluse for fear that you will be assaulted.

The memory of my childhood, is left to remind me of how backwards the world can be. It often makes me so sick, I want to curl up in a corner and die.

At age six, my job description was: sex toy.

Prayer is NOT Magic

As a child, I was deathly afraid of praying. I never thought I had the right words to say at meal time. The children's prayers were always comparted to one another. One of the triplets was always considered the "good prayer."

My sister said a bunch of *holy words,* and my a-mother would hint at how good she was at praying.

She was inferring the rest of us were not.

When it was my turn to pray (I never volunteered, I was always forced), my a-mother would "guide" me through the prayer, as though I was some stupid person. I quickly learned that my thoughts and feelings, and what I had to offer, and how I offered my prayers up to God, was not important to my APs, so why would they be important to God?

I still somewhat have this fear. I still feel as though someone is watching me, and waiting for me to fuck up so they can tell me how "incorrectly" I was praying. I cried myself to sleep many nights wondering if my prayers ever reached God's ears.

I was criticized constantly. Most of the time my a-mother would have this demanding tone that I "pray" when we had guests. That is when I hated praying the most. I hated being the "center" of attention and yet, my a-mother felt she had something to prove, or someone to show off. In front of guests she would tell me how well I did, but behind closed doors she would grunt and make odd noises, signifying I didn't know what I was doing.

Today, I think of prayer as just another way to communicate. I believe it is this ability to have a conversation with yourself. Over time, I've learned that prayer does not fix things; prayer fixes us. I can't pray for wealth, or a car, or a house, but I can adjust my thinking.

Prayer is not magic.

You don't just close your eyes, say a few words, then all of a sudden it appears before you. In my experience, nothing good comes with thinking that all you have to do is say some words and your "wish is my command." I wish life worked in that fashion, but it does not.

"For health and strength and daily bread we give you thanks today." This is our prayer as a family; my wife, daughter and myself.

We are thankful people. Prayer allows us to reflect on being thankful. However, it does not make us thankful. It creates conversations, and opens our heart and mind. For us, prayer is important, but it is not vital.

We each find our center or connection with an entity in different ways.

Growing up we were all forced to believe what *they* believed.... And in the end, it was nothing. As a child, we had all these cult-like rituals, a set amount of "prayer" time, music restrictions, required participation in church activities.

My a-mother forced me to sing in church...she never asked how I felt about it, she just assumed that she could make me do it, because after-all, she sacrificed her life for me.

She was the person we really prayed to. She told us she had the distinct ability to speak for God. I believe she thought she *was* God. When you are little however, you fall for a lot of shit.

I remember them having a particular youth group on our compound. This youth group was not a church group. But one of the requirements and stipulations was that they *had* to attend evening worship services. It was around 6pm each night (sometimes once a week depending on how long the groups were visiting). Someone protested. I wanted to stand up for that that person because I understood what he was saying.

And I agreed, people should not be forced to worship.

My APs always preached openness, yet they forced everyone to act and be like them. They had a kind of power and control over people. People were mesmerized, moved, and completely manipulated by them. They disguised themselves as shepherds when in reality they were the *star* leading the shepherds astray.

I couldn't wait to get out of that house. I think I was around 18.5 years old when I finally was able to leave. I didn't actually "leave" until I moved away to college.

I lived at my a-father's house which was about a 25-minute drive from the country. I stayed and helped him with his business. I never wanted to return to the seclusion which was my a-mother's scary haven. But she started getting jealous and though I was 18 and "out" of the house, she still wanted to have massive control over me. She phoned every day, imposed new rules each day, and required me to go and *visit* with her once a week.

Finally, I went off to college. At college I began to feel like an actual person with some independence, instead of the soldier-zombie-robot I was expected to be. But even getting into college was *her* doing. I didn't know I was even going until five days prior. She took my entrance exam, she wrote my entrance paper, and she applied for me. She had no faith in me, and believed I could not do it on my own. She chose the college I would attend, just like she chose me in the orphanage.

I had no say, and my needs did not come first. And yet, even from that distance, she controlled me…she wanted to know where I was, what my grades were and whether I was "becoming like her"- as in open-but yet closed at the same time.

In college I began to pray in a way I had never prayed before…I began to pray with purpose and I learned that my prayers were important. I learned that others wanted to hear me pray, that people actually cared about my prayers and most importantly, God cared.

Growing up, my voice was stifled…and my prayers were stunted because my a-mom believed she was the voice of God.

Just Because We Smile

"But my children are so happy. They smile all the time."

    I hear this so often. It hurts my ears to hear this. The thing is, I am not saying that they are not allowed to smile, I am saying, just because they smile, it does not mean they are "happy." This is something that really gets mixed up in the adoption world. APs think that if their kids smile, then they must be a happy child and have no trauma.

    WRONG!

    As a child, I smiled because that was what was expected of me. They *saved* me so the least I could do was smile. I only smiled because when I didn't my a-mother would pinch me or speak harshly to me. When I didn't smile she would tell me that I was moody, or that I was ungrateful. So I learned early on that smiling kept the pinching to a minimum and the verbal attacks at bay. It was always a very tense time in my home because everyone else seemed to be so happy.

    The white kids always got what they wanted and yet, I always had to share (except my bike). I remember looking at pictures of myself when I was younger and being the one who felt like she had to force out a smile just because everyone else seemed happy.

    "You opened my spiritual womb," my a-mother would always say. I hated how she said it and the fact that she said this. It put so much pressure on me as a child. How could I be responsible for opening someone's spiritual womb? If I fucked up, does this mean she can no longer be spiritual because I've closed it up? And what does this all mean? Was she NOT spiritual before she took me away from the only family I knew? How did she live her life before? Why was it my job to keep her spiritual?

And so I smiled in order to make sure that her sanity could be kept and that she could feel that she was doing "God's will" while robbing me of everything I once was.

God forbid we show up "angry" on the family portraits.

Just because we smile, does not mean we are happy.

We Don't get to Choose

September 12 2015

What would happen if children received a catalog or a referral of adoptive parent options?

Children are so fragile, especially as they become teens. But when they are real little, they don't see adoption as a "choice" for them. They live with their a-parents and learn to love them. Young children don't even realize anything is wrong with them until they are told, or until they find themselves sitting in an orphanage with other kids who also have no idea why they are there.

The "what are you in for?" question starts to circulate.

Little kids don't understand what adoption is until they are put with a family that is not their own. And even then, if the new family is not forthcoming with them, they begin to exist in a world where they feel different but don't actually comprehend why they are feeling this way. The difference could be color, hair, height, ability, disability.... but the most obvious one is blood.

See, adoptive parents have options when they decide to add people to their family. One of these options is adoption. They can look at a catalog and go "children shopping" in order to get them feeling warm and fuzzy about the idea of another child, or their first child. Or they are sent referrals by adoption agencies and this begins the virtual process of bonding with a child they have never met before.

They become "paper pregnant."

And then comes the socialization visits that many times end in tears because the new parents will be with the new children and have to leave them and return to "real life" as they may call it. And the child sits there and waits…and waits….and waits for their new mommy or daddy or both to come and get them. But why are they coming to get them? Don't they already have a mommy, daddy or both?

We did not choose to be adopted. I didn't, I know that for a fact. I can say this because I look at the life I have lived, and the way I was treated as the adopted child and think "what did I do that was so bad that my mother didn't want me anymore?" I can't shake that off my lips, and I'd love to. I'd love to just sit back and be appreciative. I'd love to thank God that I was somehow saved from my fate (which according to my a-mom and others, was DEATH).

But I didn't choose her.

I didn't choose them.

I wonder what it would look like if I had the catalog in my hand and I could pick and choose who I wanted to live with. I think that is how they got to choose who they wanted to be part of their family. And why me? Was it because I was mildly retarded (yes, slow, and functioning at a very low level)? Was it because I was four years old and still couldn't walk, or talk, or barely sit up? If I look at the photos of when I was in the orphanage, there were many like me.

Was it savior mentality? Did they choose me because I was the most banged up and they would feel better if they could "heal" my disenfranchised body? Because they didn't. A body that was once unable to express itself became a body that depended on the white man.

They went up to my crib as if I were a puppy waiting to be picked up.

"That one...I think I'll choose that one!"

Children don't get to choose. I think about my daughter who is now 12 years old. Her biological mother who loves her so much has actually been the person I look up to the most for several reasons. When my daughter was about four years old, she and her sister were dropped off at my a-father's doorstep (where I grew up). I happened to be there, wondering "what the hell does this woman want?" She had a 6-month old baby hanging off her arm, a 3-year-old and a 4-year-old. She begged me to take the children. I already had two foster kids with me at the time. My goal was to educate them, give them healthy meals and travel the world with them.

She proceeded to hand two children over to me, and I fought her by giving them back to her immediately. She began to cry, and through her tears I understood that she could not care for them. One child had heart problems and the other child was basically the caregiver-she was four when she learned how to use charcoal to cook the meals for the family when her mother was out.

"Ok" I said.

"I will help nourish them and put them in school, but that is it."

She was so happy I was going to take them that she gave me the biggest hug. She thought that I would keep them forever. She thought that she would never really have to see them again. She was wrong; to make sure she knew I was only helping her out for a short period of time, I sent her kids to her on the weekends. I sent them with canned beans, a bag of rice, their bottles, their nappies, and their favorite toys. She would have to be with them every weekend. She was not happy about that because this meant that she could not continue to do as she pleased. This went on for about 3 months. I found out one weekend that the oldest was being left alone with all the children and that there was another bun in the oven. I was not a happy camper. Here I was trying to help get these two kids healthy and functioning and the biological mother was nowhere to be found.

So I stopped sending the kids to the biological mother. I had to make a decision, send them over there and risk the 4-year-old playing mommy all weekend or keep them with me and cut out my entire social life. Not to mention, at this time I was a full time teacher. My social life had to go. I didn't feel I was finished getting the two sisters healthy so I continued. November rolled around and many changes had been made. The youngest returned to the biological mother because my work wouldn't allow me to take off more sick days to take her 2.5 hours away to the children's hospital for her heart issues. So she returned but I continued to help financially. I tried to return the older child because my intention was really NEVER to adopt her but she wouldn't go. At almost five years of age she wouldn't budge. I remember her wrapping her feet around the stool so tightly that it took me, my older foster daughter and the live-in nanny to get her off of it. When we got her off, she just ran to the couch and cried, kicked and screamed.

You see, she saw something different. She saw something that she didn't want to let go of. She saw a life that she had not seen before. Yet, she did not have the choice. She was under five years old. I told her mother that I would continue to educate her and take care of her but at some point she would have to return.

To make a long story short, she is now 13 years old and legally adopted by me. She did not get the chance to choose her adoption.

We chose for her.

Her birth mother chose to give her away. For me, I had options. I could force her to return or have her stay.

Adoptees don't get to choose their new families.

For many reasons, I chose to cut ties with my family. Many won't understand why and many may say I'm unappreciative, and many may say I'm lucky, why did I do such a thing, and others will say I'm a spoiled brat, and some white adoptive parents (WAP) may say I'm an angry adoptee, and still others will say I'm a Reactive Attachment Disorder (RAD) child and ungrateful.

YES, to all of the above. But everything happens for a reason. I didn't one day just wake up and say "I hate everyone," it all happened gradually.

As an adopted adult I find myself asking many questions. If I were asked "would you like to be adopted" I would have said "no." But that is not how it works for us, we are forced to accept who we are paired with. I don't believe that all of it is God's will.

Many adoptive parents want to label their child once things get difficult or they have decided to emancipate themselves. Not all adoptive children will be quiet and submissive (this is what my a- mother wanted). Not all children will bow down. But not all adoptive children will be destructive, angry, hurt, scared, or difficult.

As soon as I realized that emancipation was an option, I had one more label put on me. Instead of asking the "Why" questions…. they pointed the finger at me.

Instead of attempting to understand the feelings the child is going through, they pointed the finger. The berating never ended.

When adoptive parents realize and try to understand that their children didn't have the choice, the parenting styles and expectations will begin to shift in a healthier direction. The blame game stops, and families begin to embrace on a whole new level.

My prayer is that all adoptive and foster families start asking more questions and stop pointing the finger. No one is perfect but we can all work towards a better understanding of each other. I hope that APs and foster parents open their eyes to the reality that your child *didn't see a picture of you before you saw a picture of them.*

They did not choose you.

You had options.

You chose them.

Coming out as BLACK

August 1st 2015

Awhile back I spent a little over an hour watching Wanda Syke's "I'ma Be Me" stand-up routine. There is a section in this routine that made me laugh so hard that my daughter looked at me and said "seriously, whatever you are laughing at must be extremely funny…. but please, for the love of Lilly (our pet), shut up!"

Wanda was talking about the difference between Gays and Blacks. She stresses the difficulty of coming out as gay and she says that one does not really have to "come out as black" to their parents if their parents are black too. The way she set it up was genius.

It got me thinking though. When you are raised in a predominantly white Christian family, often times your adoptive parents just see you as one of the rest. You grow up thinking that your siblings who are white, are just like you, so you must be white too. You grow up not really knowing that you are black. You grow up in racial isolation.

It is not really that they did not talk about race with me, it was more of a "it won't hurt her if we don't mention it." The problem with this thinking is that everyone around me noticed, and called me ugly and morena (which is equivalent to the word *nigger*).

So, if I was hearing about my color from other people, why would my APs not acknowledge that I was indeed black?

I remember being about six years old, I came home from school very upset. I had a fight with another kid who happened to be my color. He said "negra" to me. Still, at six, I had not heard my family directly say I was any particular color. But the boy told me I was black and it made me so mad. I got home and I was sobbing intensely (the type of crying that makes you convulse uncontrollably while bouncing your shoulders up and down). I was mad. I was so very pissed that I was called black.

Why had my sister not been called black too?

I didn't get it!

My a-mother put me on her lap and said "I hate to break it to you…. but you are black." This was so devastating to me.

Me?

Black?

I thought I was…. like everyone else.

When she told me I was black I cried even more. Maybe psychologically I knew that between the ages of six and nineteen I would be treated poorly solely based on my color. So I hid. I tried to pretend I was white. I spoke "white," I walked "white," I thought "white."

I wore clothing that I thought would help me fit in.

At around age 14, I was sent from the Dominican to live with "family" friends in North Carolina. The family I was put with was completely white so I thought "yes, I'll fit in just fine." My APs told me I didn't want to be around the blacks that we saw on T.V. They were too aggressive and they talked funny. The first day I walked into school, I remember walking to my locker. I had on these Khaki slacks and a button down shirt with a really ugly sweater my a-mother had purchased for me at the Goodwill before dropping me off in the all-white world.

There were three pretty black girls at the lockers. I walked past them pretending not to notice or hear them but in my heart, wanting to be just like them.

One snickered saying "Damn, that nigga walks like she be white…don't she know she be one of us?" I remember this clear as day because I actually turned around. I opened my mouth to say something and once I started to speak, they just laughed right in my face.

That was the first time I had actually encountered black people who would expect me to be black and, one of them. I had encountered black people in the country I was raised in but I was too dark to be one of them. The lighter you were, the more refined you were. So, when I went to live in the United States, I learned that black was just black.

Each year after the age of 14 I lived in different states in the USA. I began to open up my mind, but the problem I was still finding was that I was living with all white families who associated with all white friends and went to all white churches.

I was the only black girl at the after-service potluck.

I was enjoying meeting black people at school but wouldn't dare bring my new friends to the house. I felt the families I lived with were uncomfortable with me in the house, and would flip if there were two or three of us So I continued to hide.

I was introduced to loving diversity when I was chosen to be Lionne in the off-Broadway musical Blaire. I lived in Boulder for about 4-6 months and finally learned about culture and diversity. There were all types of people there: gay, straight, white, black and ginger. It was a mosaic-a beautiful site to see and be a part of.

I was 17 years old and I belted out lines and songs and felt at the top! After all, I was chosen out of all the others who auditioned (so I was told). During this time, I had the chance to speak at a few high schools about my role in the musical. I had no idea what my role meant to the black girls and boys in school. I was their role model. But I realized after the 2nd night of presenting, that even though I was playing the part of a black woman, I had not really accepted my blackness.

I had not really come out.

It would take another 4 or 5 years before I actually came out as black. When I told my a-parents what they already knew (usually the case for the LGBT community), they were upset with me. They treated me differently because I wanted to embrace my blackness and because I had chosen to embrace it and they could no longer pretend that I was just like them. I told them that I wanted to be black and they would say "you are who you are" which for me felt like they were dismissing my new found identity.

For them, being black meant being loud, poor, in debt, full of foul language and drugs, pregnant at 15, and uneducated. Oh man, did I hear the uneducated bit way too much! So they didn't really want me to "be black" in front of white people.

I asked them why they felt so ashamed and they said it was because that was not the "way they had raised me." For them, my identity was in how they raised me, surrounded by their kind of people and now I wanted to "be black."

"You'll get tired of it" my a-mother would say. Tired of what? being black? How can I get tired of being who I am?

I learned later that what my adoptive mother meant was that I would get tired of "acting" black. As if blacks have a certain way of acting. I told her after college that I was tired of "acting" white. It shook her to the core because in her mind, that was all she knew.

I came out as black and it felt strange.

Black is not an activity or action or mentality. Black is who God made me, so thanks to Her I'ma Be Me!

If you take anything away from this chapter, understand that your children who are adopted and living in a world that is different from their own culture or race, often think that they are who they are raised by. Be there for them, listen to them, and for the love of Lilly tell them they are different and celebrate those differences!

Let them be who they are.

Dead Girl Walking

November 12th 2015

One of the scariest things about adoption is that we adoptees don't really know our history. We don't really know where we come from, who we really belong to, and what our future will look like. It gets worse. I didn't even know I was dead.

I was adopted back in 1987 by two people who, on the outside, looked loving, kind and gentle. But on the inside, spewed words of hate, racism, and superiority to anything and anyone who was not their hue.

So growing up, I always felt like the "other." I was that person they hated so much.

"Black people are this way; black people do that" is what I constantly heard out of my a-mother's mouth. I had to "talk proper" or I'd be classified as one of them. I wouldn't be welcomed.

They never directly said "White people are better" but sometimes in the not saying, you say way too much.

When I was about 10 years old, I started to develop faster than my sister. During the time I was living with them, they told me that I was the same age as their biological daughter. So up until I was about 10, we were the same height, and the same pudginess. So I really had no reason to doubt their claim.

It wasn't until I was a little over 10, that I started to develop breasts. I started asking them "Why, if we are the same age, am I developing at a faster rate than she is?" Today we know that so many factors could have caused this but what my a-parents failed to do was actually care about me and what my papers said.

Instead of looking at my birth certificate, they went with their "fantasy." It was clear on my birth certificate that I was older than she was by about 3 years and no one EVER said a word. Why? Did they want to continue what they had started?

Did they want to keep pretending that I was white, like them, that I would always weigh the same as she did, that I would always be a "happy baby"?

For the longest time, I thought my name was what it was on my birth certificate. When I become a teenager, my adoptive parents finally came somewhat clean and told me that I was actually not who I thought I was. My name was actually NOT what it was on my birth certificate, that I was older than they told me I was, and that I was actually DEAD.

In Haiti, it is very hard to retrieve documents from the archives because back in the 70s and 80s, nothing was recorded on computers. Things were done by hand, stored, and forgotten. When my biological mother dropped me off at the orphanage when I was a few months old, she left me with a birth certificate (I think). The orphanage was flooded when I was 2 and all documents were destroyed.

My APs came around when I was about three years of age (or so everyone thought due to lack of good nutrition and physical care) but I was about 5 or 6. My a-mother whom I will call *horrible lady*, was volunteering at the orphanage I was transferred to after the flooding. She saw my "need" (I was in pretty bad shape) and decided she would "save me from the mud." In order to start the adoption process, I needed a birth certificate.

So the people in the orphanage started searching for something that would "work" for me. They came across a child's birth certificate who had passed away and never had a certificate of death.

"Aha!" I can hear them saying.

"This will do. The age looks about right. Who cares about the ridiculously long name and who cares that the mother on the BC is not her actual mother. We need to make sure she claimed her daughter on her own and that there was no father involved. If she goes to search one day for her real family, she won't' be able to really "find" them."

So there you have it. A year later, I sat in my AP's house with their one biological white child. I became the *live* dead girl.

There are many issues and questions I have about this unethical adoption.

1. What happens if I search for the woman on my BC, will she think that her actual dead child is alive?
2. What happens if she wants a DNA test?
3. If I go to authorities now with this story, will I become a NOBODY?
4. Are there no records of my ACTUAL Birth Certificate with my real mother's ACTUAL name?

5. Now that I have my AP's last name (but not US Citizenship) does this mean that this dead person is really part of them?
6. Who is this woman on the birth certificate? What was she like? Am I doing her Justice?
7. How does this affect me wanting to emancipate myself from my a-family?
8. How will it affect my marriage?
9. How will it affect my daughter who was adopted from Haiti too?
10. Am I supposed to be thankful that I am a DEAD girl who now has life?

Recently, I actually thought that the mother on the BC was actually my mother. Her last name was Cyr. I had known the "I was a dead girl," part but I had thought that my BC was just altered, meaning the rest of the information on it was true. It was not until I spoke with my biological brother that I realized that ALL OF IT WAS/IS A LIE and that the woman who "gave me up" is not even my MOTHER.

My real mother's last name is LIMA.

There is a feeling of loss that comes with being adoption. It is not just a feeling; it is a reality. One loses trust, and one learns to not care anymore. But there is even a deeper feeling of despair when you realize that everything you were taught to be may be true is not even a *little* bit true.

I don't know how much my APs knew about all of this. I want to give them the benefit of the doubt. But I don't forgive them for living the fantasy of me being the same age as their white kid. Because that created a lot of confusion for me as a person in general.

Finding out that the little information I had is now NADA, makes me want to curl up in a ball, and roll back into the black hole I came from.

I have nothing and no hope sometimes.

I can't answer the positive *Whys* of my life, e.g. (why do I have a beautiful singing voice?)

And I can't answer the negative *Whys* of my life, e.g. (Why do I feel sick every day? What is in my DNA that makes me ache?)

I can't connect to anyone. I can't reach out.

My biological brother got upset with me a while ago because he claims that I don't want to meet them. First of all, I'd love to meet them but it is not that simple. I have a family, and I won't just "leave it all" to visit people I never met before.

I won't and I can't.

I got a chance a couple years ago, to meet my biological sister who swears I belong to them. There is a trust factor that comes with people telling you that you are their blood. All my life I had been lied to so what made this time any different?

My biological aunt got into contact with me and wants to meet. I'm nervous and scared but also feel at peace. But is she really who she says she is? Will she have pictures of my biological mother who died when I was 12 years old?

Is this for real?

Thankfully, my APs did make an effort to keep in contact with the lady who supposedly gave me up. We also sent her pictures of me when I was growing up. They stayed in contact with the orphanage and we returned a couple times to visit. I had no idea who she was. I just knew that after every visit, I returned home with a white lady and not a black lady. Did my biological mother know that the birth certificate they had for me was not mine?

Did she even consider me to be hers?

I am this dead person. If I attempt to find my REAL birth certificate, can I become who I really am supposed to be?

What's in a name?

Power? Strength?

Glory?

Can I have peace if I never get my real birth certificate back?

I want to meet my fake mother. I want to go back to Haiti and find the person on my birth certificate. Maybe I can be her daughter that died. Maybe I can live through her? Does she even know that her daughter died? Was her daughter put up for adoption and died from mal-nutrition?

Was this all some insane joke?

But I also want my real birth certificate. I want pictures of me when I was a baby. I want to see my real mother's name on a document that belongs to ME, not someone else. Am I living my life to be the person she would have me be?

Has someone else taken my *real* birth certificate and become me? Does this make us twins? Does this make us family? Are we sisters?
I will visit my aunt, because I want to meet her, because I want to learn more about my mother, and because I want to be that much closer to being who I am.

I don't want to be DEAD.

I want to be more alive than ever.

I want to be a LIMA!

Update:

I spoke a week ago with the lady who was the owner of the second orphanage I was in. She told me that the adoption was not done through the orphanage but privately. She told me that her orphanage and a judge had given my adoptive parents custody of me and that I was allowed to live with them, and not have to stay in the orphanage.

As I read what she was saying via Facebook chat, my heart just fell. All of this talk of "giving the benefit of the doubt" to my a-parents was exactly what I should not have done. They knew way more than they are telling. Right now, I feel comatose, I feel that I can't speak to them about this because they will just deny it all.

Wake the Fuck up Christians!

We don't need to be saved!

May 30th 2015

A loud message to my white Christian mother

I grew up thinking I was the "lucky one." Somehow, I was chosen out of the 5 hundred other kids who needed a home. So, being the "lucky" one is not fun and games. There is a sense of guilt that stays with you forever.

"You should be thankful" my white a-mother would say to me as I tried so hard not to stare her in the face. "You were sitting in your own piss when we rescued you. Your mother was so poor she could not care for you. Your brother was ill and your father was nowhere to be found."

Turns out 20+ years later I find out my father had no idea my mother had given me up for adoption.

20+ years later my brother has a visa to visit the United States whenever he wants.

20+ years later my sister is not pregnant with 5+ kids as my a-mother had originally believed.

The stigma of poverty permeates in spite of her claims.

"If it were not for us, you would be dead" she whispers under her breath, loud enough for me to hear, but soft enough for me to not pick up every single word. That always hurt me. To think that they were the only ones who could "give me life" was so hard to accept as a child. I really did not have anyone to turn to. All I could think about was getting out of that house.

Along with all the other issues going on in my life, the last thing I needed was to be told that I was "lucky." As if dice were rolled and a 12 came up. What are the odds?

My a-parents were missionaries. I use that term very lightly because I believe that though missionaries do good, they immensely fuck up a child's life forever. First and foremost, their goal is oftentimes not about physiological needs, but spiritualist needs. How can one function spiritually if they are hungry or thirsty? When they do attempt to cover the physiological needs, they create a white supremacist environment and inevitably dependency.

I remember going to the "village" and watching my mother prance around barking orders to the village people. Every village person was black, poor, and hungry. Yes, she created the village…. but she also ran it. Instead of teaching them how to run it, she, the white person, had her hands in every single jar. It got to the point where the village wanted to revolt in order to gain some form of independence and control of their own culture.

The other day I spoke to a friend who confirmed my dire situation as a 2-year-old. I along with a couple other little kids were locked in a dark room for days at a time, only to sit in our own feces and drink of each other's piss in order to stay alive. Do I remember these events? No! But these events are undoubtedly buried deep down in my psyche.

As a child you want to believe everything your caretaker is saying. I believed my a-mother. I believed that I was in such bad condition that she had to save me.

BUT GUESS WHAT, I am no longer that little kid. I am a 30+-year-old woman, with adopted kids of my own, with a partner, a dog and a beautiful house with a pool. I have 3 college degrees and several certificates. I am working on a Masters and I am HAPPY TO BE ME.............

WITHOUT YOU!

Wake the Fuck Up White Christians! We don't NEED you.

I was adopted from Haiti around 3 but abandoned in the Dominican at the age of 27 because I didn't match up to the standards and benchmarks my a-mother had laid out.

I am smart-but I always was. Yes, you helped shape my intelligence by giving me an education. Yes, you kept me clean and for the most part out of trouble…But someone else could have done that. I don't believe anymore that you were the only one who could have saved me. I am claiming the freedom of who I am, and from who you are!

My a-mother did the worst she could by not giving me US citizenship. do though. She never gave me US citizenship. So yes, she adopted me, I became an obstacle SHE has overcome, I became a petting zoo-literally and figuratively. I became someone she could put on display and say "look at the good I have done." But in the end, I remain just like my biological siblings. Limited.

She never wanted me to be part of who she is. She never wanted me to have all the opportunities in the world. She wanted me to be dependent on her, like a little black slave serving her white master. Without citizenship I am still only a little black Haitian, stuck in the corner with no food, sitting in my own filth.

My freedom to be who I will always be has not come to a halt. My new-found freedom is one *without* you physically. I am free because I am who I always have been.

Just me.

WAKE THE FUCK UP CHRISTIANS……cuz when you do, you are going to wanna take a nap because the truth is so overwhelming.

December 31ˢᵗ 2015

As I type the word "adoptee," Microsoft says I have spelled the word incorrectly. It is like the way people try to pronounce my last name given to me by my APs (who gave me that but failed to give me their citizenship). They can't pronounce it and often-times they don't even try. My first name, also given to me by APs who chose not to question the unethical acquisition of my false identity (after finding out of course), is one that I am working on erasing.

Not erasing because it is not beautiful.

Not erasing because it does not "suit" me.

Not erasing because its definition does not define me (according to my a-mom).

Erasing because it is not me and never was me. My identity is built on a person who does not exist. She died at the age of 2, or 3, or who really knows. But she lives on. Through me, through my body, through my thoughts, through my mind and heart. I force her to live on. I give her movement; I am her being.

But then who is my being?

The word adoptee is not found in my dictionary. If you take the time to right click on the word, after it has been underlined with a squiggly red line the words, *adopter, adoption, adopt* are what is offered. But we are none of these. We are adoptees and we have a voice that has forever been silenced. WE have been silent because we don't want to question the hands that "saved" us. We are silent because we don't know what truth is. We are silent because literally, nothing can come out of our mouths.

This word, that gives us so much power but yet also rips out our souls, is a word that we need to claim for ourselves. We were adopted and grafted into a new family that, more often than not, looks nothing like us. For some reason, it is cooler to be the adoptive parents than to be the adoptee.

People see adoptive parents as amazing, wonderful, and brave people.

These people sacrificed their entire life to give us this life, this new existence that our parents would have "wanted" for us. How do they know? How do they know that they would have wanted this for us?

Had they known that I would have been treated like trash, sexually, physically and emotionally violated, and become that angry adoptee that everyone talks about, they would not have given me up. Because what loving parent wants their child to be put through so much hurt? Not to mention the hurt, the trauma of being separated from those people who are your blood, your roots, your soul. The minute separation happens, your brain starts to rewire itself, questioning the reason to keep on functioning.

Mine did.

But who really cares, right? Because after all, they did give us a "better" life. I'm not sure if a better life can really be what they gave me. They lied to me from day one. Already, that "better" life has been an infraction on my very existence.

Like a loose tooth that is ready to come out, I longed for my family. I longed to be part of them and yet, something (that one little bit of flesh) was keeping me from fully experiencing them.

When my a-parents found out that my adoption papers were falsified, and I was indeed someone who was dead, they chose to laugh about it. "Well, at least we got out of that hell hole where they were parading heads on sticks."

Really? How about how I feel?

Knowing that one day, when I die, I would have died twice.

Has anyone died and been born again? That is what I will be...a born again, and a death once more. Have they ever stopped to think that maybe this "funny joke" was not fucking funny at all?

And what does all of this mean legally?

Has the dead girl's death certificate been registered?

Have I hijacked her own death?

I will never know until I die.

Will my spirit become one with hers?

Will I be tied to someone who I have never known?

Will this arranged marriage lead to an eternity of togetherness?

Am I one in spirit with her?

Will I be one in spirit with her?

Ahhh! These questions will plague me forever. Many people say "just get over it. It's going to be ok." Or they say "That is pretty cool, you gave this dead girl life."

FUCK all of you who say these things.

No, it will never be ok. There are so many legal implications of me being someone I am not.

Fraud.

And who are these people who signed these papers?

I think of those people in the US who complain of identity theft. How sad, how frustrating. You lose everything and it takes a long time to regain your identity. Ah, this feeling you feel....

I am that thief. I was not a willing player though.

I'm afraid to search for my real identity. When my brother told me that my mother's name was not the name on the birth certificate that I so inappropriately own, I fell on the ground and started to cry.

"What? How can this be?"

My a-parents told me that my identity belonged to a dead girl but they never cared to talk much more about it. Not sure if they were uncomfortable or if they just didn't care. I have no idea. I guess I should have put 2 and 2 together. But I couldn't. This 2 plus 2 did not equal four this time.

It equaled "HOLY SHIT."

Why did I not connect the names? Because I was a child and it was not my job to make those connections. It was my a-parents' job to go to the people who wrote up these false documents, and question them. They should have said "make this right, my daughter has always had trauma, the last thing she needs is to assume the identity of someone else, not just someone else, but someone who is dead." But no. They didn't question. They didn't ask. They didn't care. What they cared about was their own life....

missionaries, doing the will of God while holding hands with Satan.

I don't blame them for the unethical adoption. I blame them for making it sound like it is a "funny" thing. I blame them for not caring to make things right. I blame them for thinking I'm still that adopted child instead of an adopted adult who has a life, a wife, and kids. I blame them for being selfish and thinking only of their "saving" mission instead of their "drowning daughter." I blame them for not standing up for me.

After reading the book *Ghost of Sangju* by Soojung Jo, I realize I've had the chance to answer my own questions. It took me a bit more than three hours (over two days spread out) to read the book. The book has indeed reopened the scab and has caused tears to gush out from every orifice. My whole body cries out because my innermost being is not who it should be. A friend of mine told me I am still me. I am that "me" that I crave so much. And in a way, I agree with her. Because who else would I be? But the issue with this is that my identity is not me. My documents do not represent my soul. When and if I want to search deeper, where do I start? If I choose to return to my birth land, will I be arrested for impersonating someone?

I had this strange realization when I traveled to Haiti in August of 2015. This was the day my daughter's adoption papers were complete. This overwhelming feeling of joy, frustration, guilt, anger, and questions loomed over me like a heavy dark cloud about to rain. I hated what I was doing, and yet at the same time, I could not go "back." Her adoption was unconventional in the sense that I never planned to adopt her. I just planned to open up the door to other options for her, but I could not really do this unless she was legally part of me. The US would not allow me to open up these doors unless she was legally adopted. The

US forced me to change her last name. It dawned on me that unless I changed her last name, the life I wanted to offer her would not exist.

After the earthquake of 2010, the US used tighter security measures to eliminate abduction and child trafficking. But what about those people who are not abducting or trafficking? They are forced to create a whole new identity for the kids they wish to forge a different future for. I was one of those. I stood at the border, and watched people with broken limbs, bashed in heads, forgotten souls, rush into this semi constructed building on the other side of reality, and I was there, in my blue scrubs and afro-tastic hair, ushering my own people into a country where they are not welcome. And yet, in that very instance, racism, hatred, prejudice and superiority took the back seat. For those few minutes during my triage duty, the world stopped, my ears ceased to do its job, my eyes got blurry, the air was punched out of me, my mind was suspended between the odd belief that *dreaming while being awake was not really dreaming at all.*

And babies cried tears of utter despair as they watched their mom and dad be taken away, as they felt the cool but brief wind from a blanket pass over them as the unskilled volunteer covered their loved ones faces and bodies because death had come upon the physical selves.

I stood in disbelief, with no words, no space, no time, no mind of my own.

I understood why people wanted to take these babies. I understood why trafficking would become an issue. I understand why the US required new and stricter laws. But I was not one of those. And yet I've always felt like one of them.

My daughter, even though she came to me at age four, is one hundred percent her mother. She belongs to her mother, not to me. And yet her mother wanted me to open that other door for her because that was a door that she, at the time, was not able to open. That door needed more people as it appeared to have been made of concrete instead of a light wood that can be found as scraps on the ground on the way to work.

Finally, as I sat in Haiti, nervous, and having to pee, I was told by my lawyer that it was because of my "proper" adoption, that my daughter's adoption was approved. Does he not have any idea of how my adoption was done? How was my adoption "proper"? And then it came to me, the person I am impersonating's death certificate has not been registered. Or it has been registered but it has been hidden. A million and one questions rushed through my head. Did the orphanage not ever tell her parents that she had died? What if the mother decided to go back and visit her in the orphanage a few years later? Would they tell her the truth?

Is any of this the truth?

I had to hold my tongue as I wanted to tell him everything I knew. And at the same time, I didn't want to jeopardize my daughter's newly completed adoption we had waited 3.5 years to conclude. I was selfish, and yet I was also thinking about her and her mother. Her mother would not "take her back" as I tried when she was four and a half, five. My hope was just to give her food and schooling, get her healthy and prepare to let her return to her mom, and yet she would not let my hand go.

I shook it, I told her "ok honey, you are ready." It had been an open fostering, I just wanted to get her healthy as she came to me with red hair, and skinny legs. Her mother dropped her off (along with her 3-year-old sister). I told her "Sure," I'll get them healthy again. And that is what I did.

But she would not let go of my hand. I pulled my arms up as she clung to them. I shook, and pushed her away, tears welling up in me. Her sister went willingly; she was 4 at the time. The stay was supposed to be temporary. And yet she would not let me go. I became stern as my oldest foster daughter watched from inside the car, phone in hand playing a game but yet one eye always watching to make sure I was "safe" (she was my Larimar). But the child would not let me go.

And then I heard these words spoken by her mother in Creole "li pa pu mwe" (she is not for me). And I stopped. I got down on my knees to reach her level and said asked what's going on" in Spanish because that is the language she spoke at the time. "No quiero ir" is what she told me and gave me a huge hug. My foster daughter who was in the car yelled out the window "Mom, I'm going to be late for soccer." I had a decision to make, leave her despite what she wants, or bring her with me and unwillingly allow her to lose her language, culture and part of her identity.

"FUCK," I thought in my head. My daughter yelled out the window again, and like a typical 13-year-old, honked the horn. "I'm going to be late.... gosh!" I turned around and as much as I wanted to yell at her, I just said "coming!"

With child in hand, her mom handed her backpack back to me. The backpack had all her new clothes we had bought in the 6 months she was living with us. Her cute socks, her bottle (because she was attached to it), and her ribbon. I affixed the backpack securely on her back and her hand still remained in mine. And yet, even in that moment, I told myself that this little human being would only be with us temporarily. I told myself this as I was not ready to make it permanent.

As I think about my adoption, I think about what it must have been like for my birth mom. I was sick, I had heart problems, and I was small. My birthdate is wrong on my birth certificate, but the day of my birth is known, the year, no one seems to really know. January 21st. My APs gave me February 14th because that was the day I opened my a-mom's spiritual womb. I hated it, especially since I felt no love on a day that is supposed to be all about love. So I no longer celebrate that. My passport birthday puts me three years behind, which actually made it very difficult for me to adopt my daughter. And yet, receiving gifts at three different times was sometimes nice.

But we don't exist. I don't exist anymore. Not on paper, not in spirit, not in real life. Because maybe, I never really had a birth certificate. And if I did, how was my name spelled? Was my father on there too?

Mom, if you are in heaven (I can't imagine you anywhere else), did you really love me? Does love mean you give children up? Does love mean you trust strangers? Does love mean you didn't want me to die? Who are you to think I would die.... oh yes, you are my mom and many times, and in this situation, I believe a mother knows best.

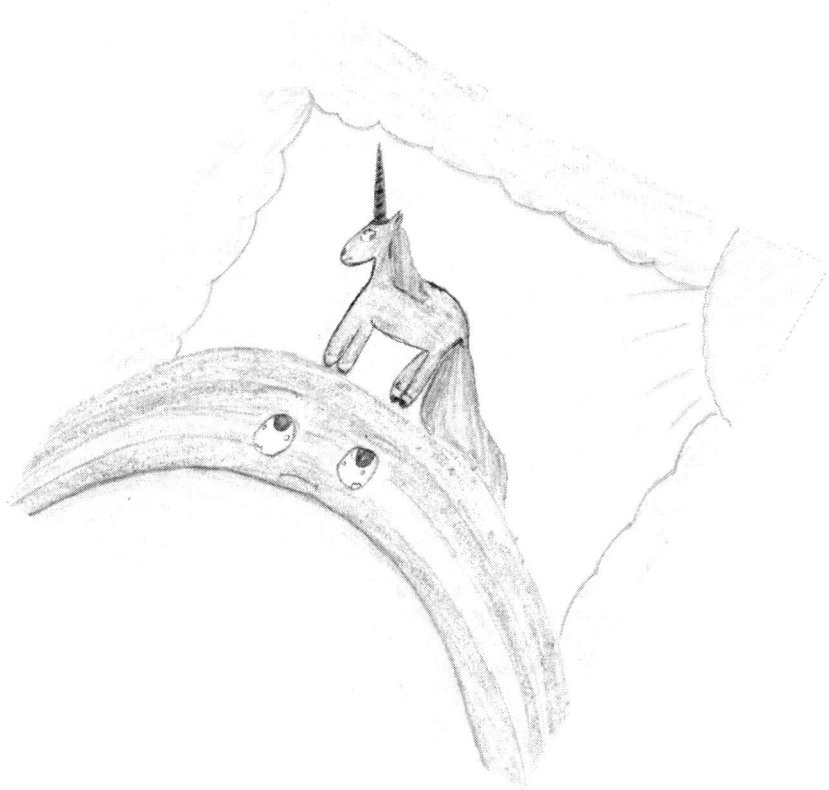

HEALING

God or Santa

I was never a big communicator; I think this is what made me explode when I become an adult. For so long my thoughts and feelings were bottled up somewhere and I couldn't open the cap. My a-mother was excellent at gaslighting. I got to a point in my life where I believed everything she said and did. I began doubting myself, thinking that the way I thought was wrong and "how dare I" think any different than she.

It was hell…every day of my life.

Except for one Christmas. I was not sure what I believed in because as kids, and especially as adopted kids, you believe whatever they tell you about your story, about who you are…about what color you are…. you are required to trust them, because they did "save your life."

I believed in Santa…and that year for some reason I walked away believing in Santa more than I believed in my adoptive parents.

I had asked for a bicycle. But I had not asked any particular person, nor had I written it down anywhere. I had it just in my head. I thought to myself "God, if you are real, then you will tell Santa that I'd like a bicycle." I remember never having told ANYONE of my desire to have my own bike and on Christmas day, there it was, outside, waiting for me to ride it. It was my very own bike. I didn't have to share it with anyone. I think I was around 11 or 12 years old when I received the bike. Did I believe in Santa or did I believe that God had really told Santa what I wanted for Christmas? Either way, I had what I wanted. It was a beautiful bike.

I spoke with my a-mom the same day and I remember being very surprised that the bike was out there. My first thought was naturally "how did you know?" And her response was "we just know." I didn't question that. I look back on that however and wonder if it was a lucky guess. But at that time, in that moment, I was happy. I was content with the bike no one was supposed to know I wanted. I was thrilled that God had answered my prayers…. for once. And I was excited to see that now I had a way to get out of this chaotic household, even if it meant for just a few hours at a time.

Death by Faith

June 8th 2015

Everyone has heard of the Biblical verse "faith without works is dead." This verse has become a cliché in the Christian community. It is said by many Christians and many non-Christians.

You can't say you have faith in something, and then sit on your ass and expect whatever you have faith in to come to fruition.

Of course, this verse was also used to divide many believers into new religious groups. So some will emphasize how important it is to do work, work, work, but only a bit of faith is needed. Another group will say, just have faith—very little work is needed.

Then there is a happy medium. Or is there even such a thing? What happens when you decide to say "work without faith is dead?" This hits home for many because this calls on and embraces every religion. It is essentially saying we all have faith in something.

We all work, with a goal in mind, with a desire and faith that what we are working towards will: feed the family, get the promotion, be gratified, be sexually satisfied, be healed, make the next car payment, pay the next electric bill, write that check for that last cancer treatment.... put a smile on a face.

Faith is universal. Something you can't see, touch or feel, just something you know in your heart, soul and mind, something that transcends any logical thought but yet is extremely logical. Faith is something that keeps our hand stretched out.... something we subconsciously teach our children, something we miraculously cannot deny. It gives us reason to live.

To breath.

To hope.

To be.

That faith is sometimes a product of our works, because in the back of all our minds, the work we do is because we have faith that our actions will yield something- beauty.

When I began writing my first book, I was only 13 years old. I wanted to document the hurt I was feeling. I wanted to write the days and times things happened to me. I wanted something to be there, physically; something I could pick up and leaf through in times of heartache.

My first book is a compilation of my journal entries. For so many of us, journaling has been something we can count on. Even though it says "private," we want the world to read it and know that we are not alone. When we use the key to open our journals, we are not only opening the journal to ourselves physically, we are allowing our spiritual and psychological self to be part of the journey.

Some of us title each new chapter "Dear God, Dear Jesus, Dear Spirit, Dear Journal." We give it a beginning middle and end. Just like our very existence, we too have a beginning, middle and end.

We give it a name because we long for understanding and a connection. We long for a connection that allows us and the journal to feel us, know us, understand us. Some chapters forget to be titled because they are the most abrupt, scary, and insecure parts of our lives.... we don't want to identify with our foundation, and yet at the foundation we yearn for an "I get it." So we don't title it, thinking that our heart, mind or body will forget that we ever wrote that part. This also allows us to go back years later and read it over, dismissing its importance; again allowing us to disconnect.

We write because we have faith that our journals will hear us. We have faith through expressing ourselves, we can truly understand our journey and who we are. We write and realize that it is through our writing that we learn that the power of faith is something that continues and is picked up, and found, and is had. Faith is not something that we are only born with, or, forced on us. It is something we have found along the way, in our suffering, in our defeat, and in our ability to conquer.

Every day we write, we lose ourselves. Writing helps us find new hope, and meaning. We work and write and pray and love because that is how we have find faith.

Faith like an object that is found after digging for days.... you have to go through so much dirt, rock, roots, mud, water, bugs, and nasty crap in order to find that treasure. Faith is like the treasure.... Faith is that treasure you have physically dug up.

Death by faith is intense. It is something you do daily. As you live your life, and smile, and love, and hug, and hope, and wish and do, do, do, you die. But as you die and uncover who you are through your story, you realize that death has brought you into something that is way better; it has brought you into faith in God or spirit, yourself, others, your friends, your pets, your accomplishments, your insecurities, your life. Each day I am killed by faith, because as I write and disclose who I am, I am dying inside.

Faith has killed me but I have also been awakened.

It leads me to a life which allows me to say that death by faith is not so bad.

Horses and Naps

January 20th 2016

When I was a young child, the way I would escape emotional, physical and even sexual abuse was by taking naps. I found that when I slept during the day, I could close my mind off to all the icky shit going on in my life. For a period of 2-3 hours, I could dream about life, love, and even happiness. My dreams were so vivid, so wonderful, and so sweet.... dreams that all children should be part of.

The minute I woke up I was off to chores again and being berated. I was used to it by the age of 13 and so I knew what to expect. The narcissistic voice, the sarcastic racist humor, the constant sexual glares...I knew it was all coming and it was all there. But for me, taking a nap put me in a world of amazement. I wished that the naps would never come to an end.

The naps put my life on hold.

My favorite animal as a child was the horse. Horses were absolutely amazing and one of my best positive memories as a child was riding them. I felt at peace with a horse. I knew how to care for them.... take them for strolls, force them into a comfortable gate....it was always fun. My a-mother used to always tell me that I was a "natural" at riding horses.

We lived on a huge farm, one that was so secluded (which made me afraid) quiet, and peaceful. At the bottom of the huge hill, you would find a grassy area, kind of like a meadow. That was where my a-parents kept the horses. I was never afraid of them, there was never any reason to fear them. I mounted them with no help as a young one and as I became a teen, road bareback all the time. One of the best memories I have was riding bareback with one of my sisters in the river. There is not a better feeling than riding bareback, holding onto the reigns, and having them float down the river with you on their backs.

This was when I experienced love, and peace and happiness. When I was on them, in the wilderness, feeling the sun on my back and the coarse skin of the horse under me, I was one with nature. That feeling of serenity...that feeling that no one can touch me while I'm up this high. That feeling of being in control but yet not knowing what the horse would do next. It was exhilarating. It was daunting, magical and spiritual. It was a connection that I could not find until I found it in nature.

Sometimes we adoptees need to find what made us happy as children. At times I can be too focused on the negative because I have always felt that there has never been closure. But if I really look deep inside myself, and think hard about the "good" times, I know there were one or two or seven.

If we allow ourselves to keep the good and leave the bad, we allow ourselves to take that one step closer to freedom. We set ourselves free with the truths we speak and the lived experiences we are able to share with the world. Hopefully by sharing, young adoptees can "skip over" the hurt and only experience what makes them happy.

Makeup and White Panties in a Twist

May 27th 2015

Growing up in this country (Dominican), I learned really quickly that I was an ugly little girl. I was not told this by my family members, but by the local people. When I left my house for a bike ride, or for a walk in the park, I was told each time without fail, that I was one of the "ugly black Haitian kids." As I grew older, that changed. But growing up I very much wanted to be white because my a-parents were white and I didn't understand why I had to be black or why I had to live in a country where being black was worse than being a dirty rat on the street.

When I was around 13 years old, I remember biking in the back streets with a child I had decided to care for at an early age. Three older boys were running after me. As I peddled my bike faster and faster down the road, I noticed that in front of me there were 4 other boys coming towards me. Both sides held sticks and rocks in their hands. I was nervous and began to sweat profusely. I suddenly had a strong urge to pee.

I was stuck.

Blocked.

I thought immediately "If only I were pretty, they would not do this to me." In some way I thought it was my fault.

My APs never let us (adoptees) put any kind of makeup on. We could not paint our toes or nails, wear eye-shadow, lipstick, lip gloss, shoes with a bit of platform.... side boob shirts, short shorts.... I was not allowed to wear a bikini until I was 18 years of age and even once I turned 18, my a-mother fought. It was not the fact that I could not do those things, it was the fact that I could not do those things until I was "out of the house," therefore making me feel even less of a growing human.

My a-parents became my first bullies, not allowing me to be who I was and feel pretty about who I was. I felt ugly and was told I was ugly every day. And my a-parents didn't help the situation. Because I was not able to "fix myself up" or "look like a girl," I looked like a black boy- all the time. My hair was often unkempt because they didn't know how to do it properly. I looked like a male rag doll.

I felt that God did not like me because I was ugly.

My white sisters on the other hand were beautiful. They were stunning (according to me). They were never chased with rocks and stones; they were never called ugly. Growing up, they never had trouble finding a boyfriend.... They were allowed to wear makeup, high platform shoes, paint their toe nails. My view of God was what I was told of Him-dress nicely, smile, look pretty. But how could I look pretty if I could not feel pretty? My a-mother reinforced the no makeup, no this, no that. No, No, No. I was to "figure it out" for myself. I felt like a nothing for so long.

When I finally was able to use makeup (once out of the house), I felt a whole new me. I realized that as I grew older, I really was not that ugly person other kids and adults would say I was. I knew that wearing makeup did not make me look like a whore like my a-mother would say to me as she compared my looks to that of a street walker. I knew that painting my nails was something that EVERY child should be able to do because that is how they grow and learn about themselves and their own beauty both inside and out. It is also just a fun thing to do with siblings.

I can remember the first day I wore a bikini in front of my a-mother. That was also the day I got contacts so that I didn't have to wear the huge glasses my a-mother would force on me. I looked like a princess…tall, dark, and beautiful.

My a-mother was LIVID. She was starting to lose control of someone she had controlled from the day she brought her home from the orphanage. She could no longer tell me how much or when I should eat. She could no longer tell me what I could and could not wear. She could no longer tell me that I was "dumb" for not knowing how to speak my mother tongue. I was beginning to detach myself from her and it felt so good.

I will NEVER treat my daughter the way I was treated. My policy of makeup at 15 has more to do with them learning and being responsible for beautifying themselves. If they want to add to their already gorgeous looks, they may but they need to be aware of what comes with it and of how to do it in a healthy manner. All girls (and guys for that matter) want to feel pretty and handsome. It is important that they be given a safe and loving environment to do so.

We have makeup in my house. And when my daughter is given more makeup, I don't grab it from her hands…. we celebrate makeup and the idea of "play" in our house. But that is the key phrase: in our house. Because she is 12, she is not ready yet for the world to see an altered side of her. She is not ready for the reactions-she deals enough with reactions from people without wearing makeup....one step at a time I tell her. Everything has their time and place.

So, as soon as she comes home from school, she goes into her room and puts on lipstick. Then she joins us in the living room and we continue with the day as per usual. She is free to express herself at home and in public but in regards to makeup, we prefer she does it at home, experiment a bit with it first, figure out what colors work on her and what colors not so much. Use eye shadow-work the shades.... use mascara, don't poke your eye out...be a girl, a boy, a person! Learn to love your body first at home, and then be strong enough to know how to respond to positive, negative and sexual comments when you are in public.

My daughter wears nail polish both at home and in public. For me, that is not a big deal. Her friends have nail polish so why can't she? She learned a while ago what colors are appropriate for what occasions. Like Bright RED is not appropriate for school. I like her to explore the colors of the rainbow and mix and match because that is part of the fun of being a preteen and growing into a responsible adult. She also makes sure that if she paints her nails, she keeps them looking clean and un-chipped. Wearing make-up inside or outside comes with responsibilities.

I want her to have the opportunities that I did not have as a child. I don't want her to feel like she is nothing until she is "out of the house." She is beautiful, smart, and has a great heart. She is something very important, from birth to death.

So, don't get your white panties in a
twist…create boundaries that help your child embrace
being who they are and who they will become…. let them
be with guidance. Because that is what is important and
that is what it is all about

<u>Cry easy</u>

July 19th 2015

I remember being a child, keeping everything in. I was so frustrated at times, I couldn't really express myself. My a-mother wouldn't let me unless she could "fix" the situation. "Just pray, lean on Jesus…. He would take it all away" she would tell me in a sweet voice at times, and other times out of anger. So I did just that. But what happens when you hold things in too long and "give it to Jesus" is that you begin to learn to stop caring, and to stop being affected. When you are a child, "giving things to Jesus" is something you cannot conceptualize. Many adults don't know what that even means so it is harder for children. It is like saying "trust in Santa."

So for me, my idea of "giving it to Jesus" was *staying quiet and not complaining even though it hurt so much.*

The first time I was molested took place in my a-father's new pool he had built for the children. We were 6 children, and I was the oldest of the children that "belonged" to he and my a-mother. I was 9 and my white sister (the oldest of the biological kids) was about 7 years of age and the other children (the triplets -1 set of twins and a biological child who is exactly the same age as they are) were 4 years old. My a-father had just poured the chlorine into the mini pool the night before and we were all pretty excited to go for a swim the next day.

I think the word excited can't be used here because at an early age I learned real fast to suppress my emotions, and how I felt about any situation. My a-mother told me how to feel. When she was upset, I was supposed to feel upset. When she was happy I was supposed to be happy. When she was sad, I had to be sad with her. Regardless of how I really felt at the time, I had to mimic her emotions. So when everyone else was happy, I didn't really know what to feel because most of the time, my a-mother was quite the opposite.

All the children were jumping up and down and my a-father said "Ok, you guys can get in." The pool, that used to be a garbage pit, was behind the house. How my a-father converted it into a swimmable space, I have no idea, but he and his handyman worked at it for months and we were all very appreciative of it. We were hot, it was hot, and swimming was just the right thing to do.

The younger ones were allowed to jump into the pool but not dive. I was too tall for my age so jumping would have hurt my legs. So the 4 year olds jumped in and yelled and screamed and had a merry time. I walked in carefully; I didn't want to slip. The 6th child, a 12 or 13-year-old at the time walked in behind me and pushed me.... I got all splashed and I remember feeling a bit upset inside. I just wanted to go in on my own.... I didn't want to be bothered. After pushing me, he rushed passed me without even saying excuse me or "I'm sorry." I backed up and sat on the step to watch the others. I can remember not having anything in my head....my mind was kind of blank, I stared out into what was the wooded area, wrapped my arms around my body because I was feeling a bit chilly. Then I took a deep breath.

I don't remember how long I was sitting there until I decided it was time to get into the deep end. I believe I had on a white full length bathing suit and my hair was afro-ed out with a headband/scarf. My a-mother never knew how to deal with my hair and all the combing hurt too much. So she left it out. Leaving my hair out was a huge cultural taboo which later led to a lot of bullying and physical abuse by my peers and other adults.

Dealing with my hair was what she called it, because combing it would be too personal and create an attachment that I feel she didn't want. Her biological children got their hair combed and the adopted/foster kids got their hair dealt with.

I started walking toward the deeper end of the pool and as I stepped into the "deeper" end, I went under water. The feeling was amazing. It was cool on my body and my hair got so wet but looked dry as soon as I had my head out of water. On the second submergence, I felt a hand on my body. I had thought that it was one of my siblings, because they were all splashing around and making a lot of noise. But I was under water and it was a bit weird.

To give you a bit of background, my a-mother pushed for a "shared" bed. For me, this was so strange, I guess because coming from an orphanage, everyone was super close in the first place. Everyone was touching each other, bumping into each other, and the smell of urine and feces was overpowering. So coming to a new home, I think I was hoping for a bit of privacy.

It was not until I turned 6 years old that privacy ceased because we had moved to a new country and my a-mother seemed to have had a change of thought. But I remember the switch happening so fast. One day I was sharing a room with my younger sister in Haiti, and the next minute, all six of us were in one big room with beds in a circle. At times she would make us put the bed on the floor and my a-mother, a-father, and her boyfriend would sleep real close to us. Yes, my a-mother had her boyfriend and husband living under the same roof. I hated sleeping so close to everyone. I felt so violated emotionally, I felt that I was not allowed to have my own dreams, my own thoughts, I had to share my most intimate times with everyone around me. I guess I was selfish as a child. But I think this is where all the sexual abuse was allowed to happen. Because everyone was so close, it justified the abuse.

So he put his hand on my bathing suit and somehow got under it on my lower parts. I remember standing up really quickly and being so confused. I was nine years old and had no idea what to think. Did I provoke it? Was it my bathing suit? Did I somehow tell him he could do that? I was so upset but I didn't know how to show my frustration.... I was angry and at the same time, the touch did not hurt, which confused me even more.

"Well, if it didn't hurt" I thought to myself, "then it can't be bad." It was not necessarily a good feeling, but it was one that forced me to realize that my vagina actually had sensations. My vagina was not just for peeing.

My a-mother never had the "talk" with the older kids. I think she assumed that we would learn as we went along, which in my opinion is the worst approach ever. My daughter who is 12 read a book called "What's happening to me," by Susan Meredith. The book actually talks to children about masturbation and how it is "ok" to feel good. I wish I had that book when I was a kid.

I remember getting out of the pool and putting on my towel. I wrapped it tightly around my body and left the scene. I went to our "shared" room and got dressed. Then, I sat on the toilet for about 30 minutes, trying to figure out what had just happened. I couldn't tell my a-parents because maybe they would get mad at me for letting him do that. I couldn't tell them because I felt so guilty, as if somehow what had happened was my fault.

I couldn't tell them because my a-mother would tell me how I was supposed to feel.

So I didn't tell them. I didn't tell them until I was in my mid 20s and even then, my a-mother would not acknowledge it. Even in my mid 20s she tried to tell me that somehow I *let* it happen. Even in my mid 20s my a-mother tried to tell me how I was supposed to feel about the situation.

The night I was molested for the first time, I went to bed scared. When I awoke the next morning I was soaked in my own urine. I didn't know if I had a bad dream, or if someone had peed on me. But I was wet, soaking wet. Surprisingly, my a-parents did not get upset with me, but when it started happening each night, until I would turn 15, anger started to become their reactions.

Our live-in maid once told my a-mother that something was deeply wrong, that a 13-year-old girl should not be wetting her bed. My a-mother didn't want to listen to her; after all, this woman was beneath my her and she had all the answers. One of the many live-in maids I would have over the next few years even told my a-mother that she had seen sexual things happening, and she would again brush it off and say things like "nah, they are just exploring, let them explore."

I cried in silence for the first time in years when I was in my 20s. I remember sitting in the hallway of the dorm room, after having the conversation with my a-mother that actually started via e-mail and I listened to her give all these reasons as to why I was molested. I ended the phone call with "I love you" because even then, I still had a deep sense that I was indebted to her.... even then she told me how to feel and I was still loving her.

I later learned, as I became more college educated that in order to be on the "good side," you start to see them as your protectors and you start to actually love them and protect them. Maybe a form of Stockholm syndrome, I'm not sure. But I felt that this woman could do no wrong. I was forced to "love" her and I allowed her to continue to tell me how I should feel, be, study, and eventually become.

My silent cries in college was the catalyst for a lot more emotions that would flood outward. I felt free because I actually told my a-mother about the abuse but at the same time I felt imprisoned because she still had control over me. I felt angry because she didn't protect me when she had many chances to.

The abuse continued (about 2.5-3 years I think-it was all a blur) until he was thrown out of the house for molesting my younger brother. But even after my a-brother blabbed, my a-mother made a joke saying "I bet he liked it." I was too embarrassed to talk about it when we had a family gathering that started with my a-mother asking "has he touched any of you guys?" He had done way more than touching me. I am thankful I didn't say anything at the time because when my brother revealed his abuse, my mother looked at him and for a second, pitied him. I knew then at about 12 years old, that I didn't want to be pitied, I just wanted my own room so that I could be away from people sleeping close to me.

She never understood why I didn't want to sleep in the same room as everyone else. She eventually let me have my "own" room-in the jungle/forest. The house was designed where there was a main house and office and all the other buildings were connected by branches with paths kind of like the Swiss family Robinson home. To outsiders it was so "cool," but to me, it made me want to puke.

Outward verses inward.

My heart became so hard; hard like a rock. Hatred for my a-mother was my focus and I hated everything about her-and yet, at the end of every phone conversation, or email, I found myself saying "I love you too" or "I love you."

I had to find a way to free myself of this hold she had on me. So I decided to write and publish my story. I had been writing about my abuse for years, in my little journal, but I decided to put it all into a book. It is my story and became my tool for emancipating my heart, mind, soul and finally body. I never meant to hurt anyone with the book, but now that the damage is done, I don't feel obligated to go through the motions.

This book has allowed me to feel, and feel deeply. Over the years I have learned to express myself and find myself crying really easily. When I watch movies, I find deep meaning in them, and I cry.

I watched *Inside Out* with my daughter and found myself seeing meaning and value in everything. I cried and cried....my daughter said "mom, this is not a sad part." And I said through my tears in the theater- "I know..."

I watched a *Ted Talk* about a photographer who took pictures of an 11-year-old girl in Seoul and eventually found someone to foster her. That story made me tear up and then cry uncontrollably in my room.

Then I started to *Ted Talk* binge....so I had to force myself to stop.

I read posts on Facebook about APs who choose not to acknowledge their adopted child's culture, people who adopt with a "savior" mentality...and a-parents who are just dumbasses and naive and think that turning their children "white" is fine and dandy because it is the easy thing to do.

I cry when I read that.

One night our puppy was eating an apple like a human and I wanted to cry. I went shopping for some groceries and an old white man was trying to help me find a cart (I knew where it was, I'm not that stupid) and I thanked him for his kindness. I wanted to cry right then and there.

There is kindness in this world and I would love to think that there is more love than hate.

Emancipating myself through writing and lifting these taboos of feeling that I can't express who I am, has been my way of giving back to the world.

If I can impact one person with my story, I know that the world will be a better place for adoptees around the world. If one child can relate, then they too will know there really is a bright light at the end of that dark tunnel.

Done with ILYs

I am on year 4…or is it year 5, and I have not spoken with my a-parents. It really is a sad situation. I think to myself, "How could this have ever happened?" This happens to other people, not me.

So as I live my life…. *sans* them…. I realize that it was inevitable. If you are a life conscious person, you would have realized, from day one, that there was trouble.

The first time I caught my a-mother with another man I about pissed all over myself. I didn't know really what was going on, I just registered that this person was not my a-father. I will always resent her for this.

What makes me resent her even more is the fact that it continued, over and over and over again. He became my father's "brother" therefore us being asked to call him "uncle," and then he became my a-mother's business partner, and then he just become a "friend" of the family. It goes on and on and what I didn't quite understand was the changing.

There was always a new role for him created by my a-mom.

I think this may have been a way to get us to not think about the sexual component of their relationship. I felt I was the only one who was aware. I was not the only one, but I am the only one who spoke up.

It was the speaking up that got me disowned. I had to. Is my life better now that I said something?

Yes.

Living a lie does not just hurt the person lying but it hurts everyone around them. I could not wake up each morning and pretend that life was fine-as they did. I could not look at this man with the same eyes, or dote on him like my a-family did.

Maybe my a-father was ok with this, and I do not judge his lack of balls when it comes to another man taking his wife-sexually, emotionally, and spiritually. However, I could not keep trying to explain to my friends why there were 2 men and 1 woman living in my house.

"Are they your parents? All of them?" They would ask confused.
"Yes, I mean…no…I mean…" I mustered.

But it was all a lie.

People divorce on a daily basis. It is no longer a big deal. Being gay does not break up or destroy the sanctity of marriage, divorce does. At least divorce, for what it is worth, is understandable.

What breaks up the sanctity of parenthood is the sneaking around, the lying and the full range of constant shit being shoved under the rug.

Living in my house was pure agony…because I felt that they didn't love me. My a-mother was always on my case about being too fat, or too dumb, or too slow…or too bossy…. oh man, does the list go on.

My a-father was rarely home as he lived in his office about 25 minutes away. My sisters were always out…doing what they do…. avoiding any confrontations or situations they found uncomfortable. And I was always grounded for not living up to my a-mother's expectations of me.

I could never please her.

So I declare today…. I will no longer love those who do not love me. I will no longer associate with people who don't help me grow. I will no longer be that shoulder to cry on. I resign myself to the fact that I will NEVER be part of my adoptive family again, as much as I wanted to a couple of years ago, even with the crap going on, I no longer desire it. I will get nothing in their will when they pass on to the next life. Things will never be the same….and you know what? That is ok!

Because the most important thing in your life is family, not liars!

My Sister by Blood

In 2013, I met my biological sister in the Dominican. I was 34 years old and I got a chance to meet her. I was working at an international school overseas and I was on my way to the *Capital* to renew my residency card. I received a call from her in the afternoon.

Wait, let's back up a bit. I had been speaking with my half-brother via social media. We had been communicating for quite some time. We have never met face to face but he contacted me in 2012. I had to know if he was just playing around and if he really was my biological brother. I didn't believe him for the first few months. He kept telling me that he was my half-brother and that they had been looking for me for a long time. For years they searched.

Let's back up even more. My a-parents had always sent my birth family photos of me growing up. I'm not sure why because they never seemed to want to talk about my real family. But they forced me to "participate" in this by making me write letters to them. One year I received mail from one of my siblings. I did not know which sibling wrote me but the letter came with several pictures. My birth family were all in the picture.

In 2008 I searched for one of my brothers online and found my half-brother. I didn't want to believe him and I didn't want to really believe that my family was still alive. My a-mother had told me that they had probably all perished during Haiti's 2010 earthquake. It was easier to think they has all passed, instead of know that they were alive and searching for me.

My half-brother and I began speaking but he made me feel so uncomfortable that I had to take a break. The next time he reached out to me was in 2012. He told me that he was trying to go to university but he needed money. He owns his own business but his business does not make very much money. I continued to keep our line of communication open but only after I forced him to prove himself to me. It took him a few days to do that and I thought to myself "this guy is trying to fuck with me and this will not make me a happy camper." I had been raised to question everything and everyone but never bring those questions to light. But question strangers? Never believe anyone. Everyone lies. That is the "truth," I was taught.

A couple days later my brother posts scans of cards I had sent the family back when I was in high school and some of the photos my a-mom had sent to them while I was in my first year of college. It had my neat letters on the cards and even my "professional" signature. I knew for sure that he must be my brother or closely related to me.

I can't explain the feelings that came over me. A man, in another country, never forgot me. He tells me the story of when I was given up for adoption. He says he does not remember much because he was little but all he remembered is that one day I was there, and the next day I was not. He says I was sick with heart problems and I was very skinny. I was a baby. A baby?!

I spent around 3.5 fucking years in a dirty orphanage often times not seeing the light of day because the caregivers did not give any care. As he told me this, I broke down on numerous occasions, crying, pitying myself, and just being angry in general. "How dare this woman not put me first" was my first thought. "Does she know what I went through living in an all-white racist family."

As I expressed my thoughts to my half-brother whose English was good enough to understand, all he could say was "why are you worrying about the past. You are alive." On one hand he right, but on the other hand he has no idea how I feel and he has no right to tell me how I should feel. I have never told him how he should feel about this whole thing. But then again, I have never asked, to this day…I'm afraid he will be an angry mess and right now, this is MY truth and I'm the only one who can be the angry mess.

So I have yet to ask him about how he feels. But I have a feeling that he will be the "loving" man most Haitians are. They embrace, they accept and they don't allow the past to define their future. But me, I was raised by white Americans who told me I would have had no future if it were not for them. So I control our conversation by not allowing him to be emotional.

We keep up communication for over a year. He asks me to buy him something via amazon and I do, but he sends me money via western union-so he is not trying to use me. He asks about university and stuff so I offer him different sites online that can help him. His English is good enough (business-like) but his messages are cold. One day I got to do a Facebook video with him. His camera was not working, but he could see me….it was strange and yet exhilarating at the same time. I wanted to know more…. but as I asked him for more, he got angry with me. He told me that the only thing I wanted was information, but I didn't want to know family…. I was upset with him again and told him "how dare you make things obvious." I was not ready for the physical meeting. I was not ready at all. In fact, this proves it. He gave my contact information to my sister, his half-sister and on a spur of the moment, she crossed the Haitian border over to where I was living.

It was a day where I was in the capitol, working on my residency card. I got a call from her at around 3pm. She got a passport, paid the 275 dollars for a Dominican visa, and crossed the border to find me. How she could find me, I don't know. The country is so big, there are many people who look similar to me and she didn't speak Spanish.

As I spoke with her in my broken Haitian, I asked her why she had come and why this was not planned out before. Me, being raised in a family where things need to be "thought out," or just me being who I am, needed details before a visit. I was upset and scared and annoyed and frustrated and blah. I became selfish again. What am I supposed to do? How am I supposed to put her up? I was only in the capital for two nights because I had to get back to my daughters and partner on the North Coast. The phone cut off and I didn't hear back from her until I reached my hotel. This time a Spanish lady was on the phone. She spoke perfect Creole and she was translating what my sister was saying. She told me that she would put my sister up but that my sister really wanted to meet me the very next day. I thanked her for her kindness and asked her if this is the number she can be reached (a dumbass question on my part. I was being a prick but I think I was just too scared). She told me that that was the right number and that she would be waiting to hear back.

I unpacked my little suitcase and got out my laptop. I immediate messaged my brother and proceeded to ask him a million and one questions. He told me (in all caps) that she was dying to meet me and that he had no control over her being on this side of the island. I told him he had all the control. Who gave her my information was what I wanted to know? He admitted to giving her that. I asked him why this could not have been done in a better way. Then he said something that has stuck with me forever.... "a better way for who? You?" And I stopped writing. I just stared at the screen, *tears streaming down my face* like in that song by Snow patrol.

"Are you there? Hellooooo?" I saw in the corner of my left tear-filled eyes.

I shut my computer screen and didn't reopen it until I returned from my shower the same night. I needed time to think, I needed time to process what I was going through. What he was going through. I needed time to ask myself questions that I had never really asked myself before. I just needed time.

On one hand I was so skeptical of this new found information and on the other hand I wanted to embrace it, but at what risk?

Before bed I got back online and called my partner on skype. I talked to her about how I was feeling and what was going on. She did what she does best, listen and then she said "give it a try." So I got back on the Facebook chat with my brother and said "Yes…. I am here." His reply:

"Big Kiss for you sister." Even when I was so hurt and confused, and angry, he still embraced me. It didn't matter what I had done wrong, his arms were always open for me. Even though he will never know what it feels like to lose a culture, language and tradition, I had to give him the benefit of the doubt. He is my half-brother. He knew what it felt like to lose a sister.

I ended my chat with him by letting him know that after I did what I needed to do, I would meet with my sister.

The entire morning was a blur. I called the night before (right before bed) to let them know that I wanted to meet up with both of them-my sister and her new found friend-the translator. They were overjoyed.

I was overly scared.

I didn't eat breakfast as I don't eat when I'm nervous. Nor did I eat lunch for that matter. I went to the immigration office and spent about 2 hours waiting for things to be completed. I then called my taxi dude and had him take me to the address that I was told to go meet my sister. The taxi dude (an old friend of mine), was so kind and he actually talked me through the encounter. We decided to meet at a somewhat mutual location and I would buy everyone lunch.

Holy fuck! This woman was absolutely gorgeous. For the first few minutes I was so jealous. Her skin was so light (you would think she was part white) and her facial features resembled mine. She had the silky-curly hair, the high cheekbones and the beautiful lips. We both seemed to inherit our height from our father. We were both around the same height. I didn't take pictures? Why? Because I guess I didn't think it was something I wanted etched in my brain forever.

But it is etched…every moment.

I stepped out of the car and she gave me a huge hug. She called me by my birth name, not the one my white APs gave me as they attempted to change my identity and my essence. She called me by my birth name and it was beautiful. She hugged and kissed me…I had no clue what I was actually feeling in that moment, except for speechless.

I spoke with the translator and she proceeded to talk to me about my sister's plans. Her plan was to move to this side of the island, find a job and bring her daughter. Her daughter? I had a niece! That feeling is amazing, to know that there are more of ME's running around. I asked her how she planned on doing that…. again, me always the diplomat. The translator told me she was hoping I would help. Then my heart dropped. They wanted money from me. I was sucked into a "trap." And then it hit me like a ton of bricks. "They wanted a new start and I was their key."

I was in the process of adopting my daughter who was 10.5 at the time. I didn't really have the know-how nor the finances to help a whole family start a new life. And immediately I defaulted to "let's do a DNA test, is this for real?" Is this person really who she says she is? But I didn't verbalize my thoughts because I thought it would be a huge insult to someone who had taken the 8+ hour bus trips to meet me for the first time as adults. So I didn't say a thing. I didn't ask for a DNA test though that is what I needed at the time. But for the first time in a bit, I stopped thinking about me.

We ate our meals in somewhat silence. In Haiti you eat in silence.... low voices. But I couldn't help but ask questions and she was very happy to answer them. After our time together (I had a bus to catch to go back to my daughter and partner), I told her I would stay in contact. I even invited her to the North Coast without thinking it through. I gave her a huge hug and a kiss goodbye and all I could think was "holy shit-fuck." I just met someone I had always been related to but have never known. The feeling was enormous. It was as if I had won that Mario level with the dragons spitting fire at me, and I managed to duck the fiery judgment. You know that feeling that at any given second, you could fall and that obnoxious "death" sound makes you want to just give up? Yes, that is how I felt.... but as I moved forward in that very hard level in my life, I beat it.

But did she?

Did my sister get what she came for? She wanted to see me, yes, but she also wanted to start her life over again, learn to speak Spanish. Get a job, and also, bring over my niece. Will she get to do this?

The short part of that is no, not if I had anything to do with it because I chickened out once I got home and entered my comfortable abode. I was comfortable, and was not at a place in my life to bring home a stranger. It's not that I couldn't, it's that I wouldn't. I felt there was already complications in my life and in my daughter's life. I didn't want to bring in a woman who no one really knew...not yet anyway.

This has left me in fear of meeting the rest of my family. What did my sister say to the rest of her family when she went back to Haiti?

My Belief

Many new adoptive parents may look at my story and think "wow, she is ungrateful, she is not thankful." And to those thoughts I will say Yes, you are correct. I ask myself what should I be thankful for? What should I be grateful for?

Should I be thankful that I was "saved" from the mud of Haiti's soil? Was I really saved or was I an experiment, a project, a mission's trip, a prize, a gift, a fetish? I see the word *save* to mean creating a safe haven for those who were in a tough situation. Which means, they should not experience the pain and suffering in their new surroundings.

Many children are adopted and treated like slaves. Many Christian families adopt for the wrong reason "God told us to adopt." I hate this reason for adoption. #1, these people believe that some invisible entity is telling them to take in a child-essentially, removing them from what they know. #2, these people are blind to the fact that you can't adopt because someone or something told you to do it. You adopt because your heart, mind, body and soul are somewhat and somehow ready to bring a child into your home.

Much of adoption is just that-the idea that God declares and the people act. My a-mother used to say that I was born of her spirit. That is a lot for me to handle. I feel there is a huge sense of responsibility. If I mess up, her spirit is therefore ruined.

Being born of the spirit is also a huge insult to those who were not. I think of my sister who is their biological child, she was *just* born of the flesh. How good must she feel to just be born of the flesh as opposed to being born of the spirit? She must not feel very special. There is something irritatingly gross about being born of the spirit. It may be, to me, the idea that God put a baby into a 13-year-old virgin and declared it "holy." Being born of the spirit to me means that God removed me from my real parents and put me with people who had no idea how to care for me.

I believe the reason we create fantasies is so that we can escape reality. Those who have not struggled in life, or have had it easy, want the fantasy to continue in this fashion.

Those who have had to suffer, realize that a fantasy is just that; a fantasy.

How does it feel to be adopted?

November 6th 2015

As a child I could never understand what it meant to be adopted because though I was experiencing it, I had no one else really to speak to about it. Being adopted comes with many questions and when you add the word "feel" you are adding a whole other layer to this very complex family life we call adoption.

Personally, adoption can embody many different feelings because it really just depends on your environment. If you are the only child in the house, and adopted, you are going to feel slightly different than if you are in a house with more siblings who are also adopted. But if you are the only one adopted, but you have siblings who are not adopted, you are walking into a lifetime of judgment, joy, pain and hurt.

Let me explain.

I was 3 years old when I was adopted by Americans who had one biological child of their own. As a black Haitian, there were several things wrong with this picture. First, the color. Though I was living in a country of my own color, I was living with an adoptive family who did not share my hue. How does it feel to be adopted? It feels as though I was out of place.

As I got older and adjusted to my new white life. I learned to speak the language well (with no accent) and I was grafted into a lifestyle that I would otherwise may not have known had I not been adopted by this family. How does it feel to be adopted? I want the accent I lost. Part of me was lost. My brain was reshaped and reformed into that of my adoptive family. I lost my language, my culture, and who I was. I was becoming white. I was leaving behind my DNA-the instrument that brought me into this world.

As a teenager I struggled because I was not afforded everything my siblings were. The biological children definitely had first choice and their voices were heard; *all the time*. I was expected to be silent, thankful and grateful. My a-mother had it in her mind that as a black girl, I was strong and I could take certain pain better than her own children. So I was treated as though I "could do it." How does it feel to be adopted? I feel marginalized, judged, and held to a higher standard with more expectations because of my color.

In college I thought I was white. And in reality, I probably was one of the whitest black people there. My a-parents wanted me to go to a "diverse" school and at the same time, they didn't want me to be diverse. They didn't want me to learn to think for myself. They wanted me to shut up and obey. I remember bringing home a "C" in one of my classes and they threatened to pull financial support. My sister who was in college at the same time was bringing home "Ds" but she was coddled and told that "it was ok." How does it feel to be adopted? It feels like I owe them something for putting me into college, for giving me a life that I otherwise may not have had. It feels like I will always owe them my life as they supposedly *saved* me from the mud.

I found out I was adopted pretty quickly. It is quite obvious when you're a-parents are white and you are not.

All it took was a look in the mirror. All it took was my a-mother saying to friends and family "and these are my natural kids….and this is…." Was I not natural? Maybe I was good friends with an actual stork. They did try to keep in contact with my birth family but at the same time, they didn't care…or they thought that I didn't care. I always felt scared to voice how I thought about them because I was afraid of upsetting my narcissistic a-mother. So I never said anything. How does it feel to be adopted? It feels conflicting.

My birth mom died when I was a teenager and my APs told me one day at the dinner table. I cried, but not much. I didn't know her. After all, she was just my birth mom. Nothing more. But I wondered time and time again where I got my looks. Why were my eyes so small? What was up with my high cheekbones? How does it feel to be adopted? I feel as though I am disconnected and not able to function until reconnected to the socket of life.

It feels unreal.

I found my biological siblings over Facebook in my mid to late 20s. I was afraid at first and thought "Oh my gosh, is this a horrible joke?" My a-mother had told me that they all had perished in the 2010 Earthquake in Haiti. How she knew that, I don't know. She always claimed she was God's right hand woman. I spoke with my brother for a bit then had to take a break because it was overwhelming to think that a small piece of me wanted to reconnect. They were alive and wanted to know about me; the one who "got away." To prove he was my sibling, he took pictures of letters my a-mother had made me send him when I was a child, and uploaded them to Facebook. I knew there was no doubt that he belonged to me. How does it feel to be adopted? I feel unbalanced, uneven, ultra-curious.

Part of being adopted is becoming one with a family who will love you forever and in return, I would love them forever. As I grew up, I realized that maybe I will not love them forever. Too much hurt, too much pain, too much judgment. Too many expectations have landed me in a ditch I can't seem to dig myself out of. Every infraction and maltreatment has made that ditch deeper and deeper. Without a ladder, there is no hope. But I did find hope; I found hope in my own children I fostered, and eventually adopted. For every time they called me "mom," I was able to climb one step higher up that ladder until eventually I was out of that diabolical hole. How does it feel to be adopted? It feels like being in a black hole.

Being adopted comes with not knowing much about your past. And when your APs choose not to share it with you, you are even more in dim silence. I came across my adoption papers as I was trying to find a copy of my birth certificate and I found the case study. As I read through it I saw a section that talked about my mental state, my physical state and my emotional state and how I should be cared for in order to improve all of the above. But that is all I know about my medical history and I am finding this out now? I feel scared not knowing anything about my medical history. What will I pass onto my biological children if I choose to have any? Instead of helping me through these temporary setbacks, my a-parents made them so much worse by withholding food from me, telling me I was fat, and physically comparing me to their biological children. My a-mother psychologically abused me by forcing me to believe that she was God's right hand lady. When I was sexually abused by other foster children who came and went, my a-parents looked at me as though I "wanted" it. How does it feel to be adopted? I feel like a pushover, a doormat, insignificant, and slow.

As an adoptee I feel I have a sixth sense (I believe all adoptees do) because I learned to be hypervigilant about my looks, my feelings, and just about everything else. I learned to answer correctly so as not to cause a stir. But I also see through people. When I love, I love deeply. When I am angry, my anger seeps out of me. I learned for so long to keep it in. I learned for so long that I was the "lucky" one and that I should be thankful. The funny thing is, I am thankful. I am thankful that I am alive and I am thankful that I serve a mighty God. I am thankful that I can speak about my experience and help APs all around the world become aware that people like me do have a voice. How does it feel to be adopted? It feels wonderful. It feels horrible. It feels complicated. It feels confusing. It feels sad. It feels like I don't just live on one side of the tracks. I live on the tracks themselves. It feels like a breath of fresh air as I am able to open my eyes, connect, relate, and understand not just those who are like me, but those who are not.

It feels REAL!

Heaven Crashes into Earth

January 24ᵗʰ 2016

Me: Hi Ella. I just want to apologize for how I behaved when you were growing up. I'm learning that some of the things I did hurt you and your family and I did not respect them and I apologize for that. I hope you find it in your heart to forgive me. I love you very much and am learning more and more about how to change. I'm becoming a better person. I promise.

I never considered my children's birth parents while raising them. I didn't really care about their feelings. In my mind, I was doing what was best for the child. In my mind, I was saving the child from a horrible situation. In my mind, I was protecting them from all that "could happen if they stayed."

I was, and still am a selfish woman who really does want the best for the children she is raising. And at the same time, knows that she can't go back and undo it.

I was raised by white people who always told me that if they had not adopted me, I would have probably died. So I grew up with this mentality, thinking that if I had not taken my kids in, as foster children, they would have become pregnant or worse, they would have died.

Regardless of whether this was true or not, the way in which it was handled was extremely damaging. This put the birth parents in a place of distrust, and unequivocal inability. I can imagine this made them feel uneducated, unloving and unable to provide for their children.

Regardless of how they felt, I didn't care. At 25 years of age, I fulfilled my promise to a little girl whom I had bonded with since the day she was born. She was my Larimar (rare and precious stone) and I had made her a promise that once I graduated from college, I would return to her and be her second mom. Except in my mind, the word "second" was not part of the equation. I wanted to be her only mom because somehow, I thought I was better than her actual mom. Due to many factors, I thought that I was more important, smarter, and more equipped to raise a child.... albeit on my own.

And so I did that. I made "good" on my promise and the minute the plane landed, the first thing I did was call this child over the phone. She was 10 years old at the time and the connection I had with her was so strong...one that I can't really describe so I tried to write about it in my first book. She was my savior in a way. She came to life just as I was dying inside. She gave me a sense of purpose, reason, and she gave me the strength to essentially forget about my trials. I felt she was my gift from God-literally. After being abused over and over again, she was the one I clung to.

She came to me after the teen who had abused me was taken back to his home forever. They said that they no longer wanted to see him and that he was not welcome at our house anymore. My brother had reported him, telling my a-parents that the teen had forced his penis into his mouth on numerous occasions. At first, my brother was not believed. They thought he was making it up. But then one day the boy looked at my white sister in a "come hither" manner and it immediately scared them. They got rid of him fast. Why they didn't believe my black brother, but feared abuse of their biological child is lost to me. But either way, he was gone and there would be no more sexual abuse on me or my brother.

But my daughter was born about a year or so after the sexual abuse stopped. And I was stuck to her like birds to a feather. I cared for her, bathed her, spent endless hours with her. She was little, and got used to seeing me, and she got to know me. I became her god-mother as is common in Latin countries. She and I were inseparable. My heart broke though when my APs sent me to the US for one semester at a time over a period of 4 years. I felt I was losing that connection with "my" child. But each year I returned, she remembered me and we picked up where we had left off-as if nothing had changed. All of my allowance I had saved up went to her clothing, and bottles and shoes and special outings. I was ridiculously and even unhealthily attached to this child. So leaving her each year broke my heart.

And then College came and I had to be gone for longer periods of time. Each time I returned though, we picked up again where we had left off. I promised her that I would always return. And I did. When I graduated, I returned for good. I returned to live and work where my daughter was and I was determined to make sure that she receive the best education she possibly could. The school she was attending was already being paid for by me, but the education was so poor even though it was a private school. As far as I can remember, she had never gone to public school because I would not allow it. Already I was exhibiting control issues and she was only 5 and 6 years old.

Looking back, I realize how little I trusted her parents. I realize how easy it was for me to feel superior to them. I realize how much I wanted to be her entire mom, not just one of her moms. The more I think about it, the more I hate myself for being THAT person.

When she was 10, they gave me custody of her. If she was going to live with me more than just part time, I needed custody of her to be able to add her to my health insurance and to permit her to go to the school where I was teaching. I had to be her legal guardian to be able to give her the benefits she may not have received had I not been her legal guardian. Yes, it is complicated...it is always a complicated mess.

But I used coercion.

I had no idea that I was using coercion but I was very familiar with manipulation in general. All my life my narcissistic a-mother manipulated me into thinking and doing things I would not have normally done on my own. But this coercion thing is new to my brain.

When we went to court, I had my a-father go with me. We were dressed professionally and I had hired a lawyer who would represent us. My a-father is a prominent and well known doctor in our town and he also was known to "help the poor." He was also very helpful with her family, providing medical aid when necessary and lending money whenever they needed it. My daughter's father actually worked for my a-father. So we (I) used this to my advantage, not realizing that they really had no choice in the matter. Their clothes were tattered and torn, they could not afford a lawyer nor do I believe they knew they could have had one.

Of course they wanted their daughter to have a life they could not provide for her, but they also just wanted their daughter to be with them. They wanted the help, but wanted her to physically be with them. They mentioned this to the judge but the judged ruled in my favor due to the pressure I now know I put on everyone.

My daughter even had a chance to speak to the judge and she too was convinced and blinded by my coercion. She was 10, and didn't understand what was going on but somehow I had convinced her that living with me was better. Regardless of what was true or not, I had managed to manipulate the entire situation.

I now had the daughter I had always wanted to raise, not considering in any way shape or form how this would affect her parents. As she got older however, she started to realize that the *once every 2 week visits* with them was not enough. She started to ask me for more time with them and I become skeptical and hurt.

I started to think she didn't want to be with me anymore. She wanted what they provided which was lack of discipline, and more freedom. They also loved her very much but I never saw that before. I only saw how the way they would raise her would allow her to get pregnant.

What we experienced together included all of this. She had definitely stepped into the world of partying and having boyfriends behind my back and I wanted to blame someone instead of myself. So I blamed her birth family for allowing her to sneak out when I had entrusted her to them on the weekends.

They really did not know how to raise a teenager but neither did I.

When she was 14 she started talking to a man (22). Often times in these cultures, it is quite normal for a poor family to give their child away to an older man with the hope that they will care for them and make sure they are fed. So her family was ok with it. When I found out however, all hell broke loose.

I continued to limit her time with them more and more and it was causing more strain on my relationship with her. I feared that the more time she spent over there, the more "unruly" things she would learn. But I think back and though it may be true, my biggest fear was losing her completely.

There were so many things I did that did not respect her culture. I cut her hair. That is something I never chose to look at in respects to culture. I did not respect the culture in which she was raised and I did not respect her parents. What I did was what I thought was right and didn't consider how they felt in the end. Her grandfather passed and her birth mother begged me to baptize her child because she feared that the child would go to hell if she all-of-a-sudden died. I didn't respect her; I was not raising them catholic because I was not catholic. I didn't respect her family tradition, religion or heritage.

I'm sorry for all of this.

And what happens when people begin to say sorry, heaven opens up. I'm not really one to believe in a heaven or really hell, but I do believe that we can choose to make our world we live in hell, or heaven. When you say "I'm sorry," you allow heaven to invade the world you live in.

I was feeling so pained with the way I had treated my oldest daughter's birth family that I finally gathered the balls to apologize. I didn't apologize directly to them, but I did apologize to my daughter. I apologized because I didn't respect her feelings about the whole thing. I apologized because I tried to make her into a mini-me. I apologized not because I wanted a better relationship with her, but because I wanted her to know that I validate her feelings now more than ever and that I had not when she was younger. I want her to feel whole. I have not taken the step to apologize to her birth family yet, but I promise I will!

When you apologize, things are different.

Heaven literally comes to earth when you humble yourself and say "I'm sorry." There is a weight that is lifted off your shoulders not because you realized you were carrying it, but because you realized you couldn't carry it any longer. Some people will learn to do better and still choose not to actually do better.

My Facebook friend B. Collins, writes about her life as a birth mother, (I asked permission to add her to this chapter). Every time I read one of her posts and blogs I think to myself "how can I apply how she is feeling to what I have done or am doing as an AP, right here, right now?" And it is amazing how much I learned from her blogs. And there are so many other birth parents out there who share their heart.... they share it because it helps them, but they also share it because they are hoping it helps us see, touch, hear, feel, and taste what they have been through and are going through now... today.

The continued WhatsApp conversation with my daughter (we live in two different countries now) went as follows:

Ella: Mom there is nothing to worry about I love you as well and I am very happy about you. Forgive me as well for everything.

Me: I worry because I want to make things right. You were a child and you did what children do at those ages. So you are not responsible for your actions when you are a child. I was an adult and it's my responsibility to show you love and sometimes I did not and I'm sorry.

Ella: I understand your point mom but you have to understand that you were alone and young and after all, you always wanted the best. It is true that I had some hard times but I learned to forgive and to let things go.

Me: I'm learning too. You are much stronger than I was at your age. I'm glad I'm one of your moms.

Ella: Thank you so much mom and I am proud of you too!

Ell is now 20 and Pearl is 12. As I raise my 12-year-old daughter, I've made many different choices in order to not repeat the same mistakes. I hate making mistakes, but when I see that I have failed, I try and do better. It is who I am as a person and it is who most of us are.

When I apologized, heaven came crashing into this sacred place I've called my soul. There is something about an apology that changes the way you think, and go about your day. It is not about whether that person actually forgives you back (though it helps), but it is about surrendering yourself to something that has kept you safe and comfortable for so long.

See, I've always felt as though I was the better person...but in the end, she was. I want to continue to experience that heaven with her, as it seems as though she found it before I did. She saved me and when she said she forgave me, more of that heaven became part of my life here on earth.

Because when you say "I'm Sorry", heaven crashes into earth.

"It didn't happen that way," I continue to hear at the back of my mind. So I learn to believe it. I learn to believe that everything I "imagined" was just that, part of my imagination.

But it is not my imagination. I know that what I experienced as an adopted child at the hands of white supremacists was real. Do you know how I know it was real? I know because as I sleep- I shake; I wake up due to night terrors (not just bad dreams). I know because there are certain smells that trigger these horrible memories. Someone could say something a certain way and I can very well fly off the handle.

It is not in my imagination because photos can tell stories that last a lifetime. If I were to put all my pictures together, they would tell a very scary tale…. kinda like the bible tells.

The Old Testament is full of stories of a God who loved his people and yet so much devastation, so much hurt, so much destruction. The Old Testament is not a G rated book, nor is it really appropriate for teens as it includes so many things that could cause fear. Think of Job. That was a test of a lifetime. Imagine having everything taken from you…. did Job really "love God that much." I don't know.

What about Abraham (I do believe he may have been on some hallucinogen) and his relationship with Isaac…really? God told you to sacrifice your son and then in the end was like "just kidding-you da man!" That is some complicated shit to think about.

How about Lot who offers his daughters up to be raped in Genesis 19:30-38. That is insane!

People try to draw pictures that match Biblical stories and I feel that they never can really capture the essence of the tale. You need to be in it to capture these, and somewhat understand what is going on here.

But people see what they want to see. People like to pretend that stories like in the Old Testament are not really "real" and that they are just stories. Or they modify it to fit their needs.

This is what they do to adoptees. As I piece my life together, through pictures I realize how all the things I've been feeling, all the insecurities, all the frustration, all the anger, all the hatred, is all VERY real.

I use to believe that maybe I *was* exaggerating.... that maybe the big ass glasses my a-mom had me wear were too dirty for me to really see or know or feel what was going on. But glasses help you focus in on the outside world, they don't really help you with the inner turmoil you may feel on a daily basis.

It was the little things, the little things that I could not control as a child that led up to my first book. I read a quote by Anne Lamott that says: "You own everything that happened to you. Tell your stories. If people wanted you to write warmly about them, they should have behaved better." And I think it is so true. Don't hang up your own dirty laundry and then get mad when someone says "hey, you are hanging up your dirty laundry."

"You see through different eyes" my a-mom would say.... she would say this to make me feel as though the lenses I was looking through were broken.

My "different" eyes to her meant I was wrong. I was always wrong. The only time I was right was when it made her look good.

Was I a critical adult when I grew up? YES. I never was able to express myself as a child. I was not allowed to. That would mean I was being defiant. If I had an opinion, it would most certainly have to align with her thoughts-never my own thoughts. In fact, I had no thoughts of my own.... I just wanted to escape, leave my "awesome" family and go somewhere the birds could sing sweet lullabies in my ears forever.

I wanted to be part of that world, the world my white sister lived in where everything was perfect. Her blonde ponytails, how they hung symmetrically on either side of her round perfect face. Her green eyes that all the boys loved. Her smile, her skin color, her sense of "everything is wonderful" was what I craved.

And yet, she was not the one waking up in her own piss wondering why this kept happening night after night. I could never be her. I could never be beautiful the way the world judged beauty. I would never amount to what she can accomplish.

I'm begging for my US citizenship...I begged my a-father to sign the Affidavit of Support so that I can try to Adjust Status....and he still failed to sign, instead he wrote a pretty nasty letter stating why he would not sign it.

Why am I begging for something I should already have? Why must I ask for him to sign something he should have done when I was a young child? But I do, I beg because I feel that he owes me that much. The real reason he won't sign it.... it's not that he can't afford it, it's that he hates me for pointing out that my a-mother was airing her dirty laundry. That is the real reason. He is being vindictive. Oh the pain…the thought that once again I could not fulfill "their desire" for me. For me to be adopted and brought out in front of people and other white missionaries as a treasure…as a toy….as a prize won at some Jungle where heathens are supposed to resemble monkeys.

It's unbelievable the amount of times I think of myself being locked in that dark room because I "talked back" but when my white siblings talked back, the dark rooms were all occupied. I can't begin to shed that layer of onion. It is too thick to penetrate because penetrating means I would have to be open to the outside world.

When I was 14 years old, I was sent to live with a very conservative Christian family. I spent about 5 months in North Carolina and I finally felt that freedom was coming my way. I had a counselor to speak with but found out later that everything I said was reported to my a-parents. So I stopped talking. Instead, I picked up a new hobby-cutting.

Just a little bit though. I didn't want to die…. just yet…all I wanted was for someone to listen to me, to hear me out. I didn't want pity, I wanted an ear.

I told the "sister" I was living with in NC about the sexual abuse I had endured as a young child and she had nothing to say. She just gave me that look-the one you give when no one has anything to say. I was 14 and she was 15 so maybe *awkward.* Again, I felt as though I didn't belong.... the truth I was living.... I wish it had been a lie. So I cut a bit deeper the next day.

As I kept cutting I realized that it made me feel more alive than ever. I didn't cry often, because I learned really quickly that crying made me look "ugly" and so why do that? How dare I look ugly in a perfect looking family. I had to be the happy adoptee.... I had to be the thankful adoptee.... I had to remember that I would have died had I not been adopted by them.

Cutting gave me some semblance of control over my own life. I got to control how deep or how wide I cut. I got to decide whether the way I cut myself would be slanted, vertical or horizontal. And the best thing of all was I got to decide whether cutting would make me cry or not. Finally, I could say I was the boss in just a small area of my life.

My truth is my truth, because I lived the experiences I remember because of night sweats and terrors, by triggers no one would really think were "triggers" and by hundreds of pictures of me being forced to smile when I had just been pinched for NOT smiling. I remember these things, I see them in my mind and I get a strange feeling at the pit of my stomach when they all come back to me.

"You don't remember that, you were only two years old." Oh but yes I do my friend. It is amazing how much children glean from what they are told. It is always strangely amazing how you can feel something that you never knew you could feel.

I found out from my orphanage that I was one of the handfuls of children who was put in a corner closet for days and weeks at a time with no sunlight and no food. I would be "revived" and swimming in my own filth. I didn't know that I was ever in this situation but my dreams told me I was. I felt them, like it was happening to me then and there. After that information was communicated to me, I realized "holy fuck," it is no wonder I struggle with this, this and this....

And yet now, the place I feel the calmest is the closet. When I am upset, or hurting, I find a nice dark closet and close it up....it is my safe haven, it is where I can sleep, sleep for days on end.... never to be awakened again.

But I'm always awakened because the night only lasts 10+ hours and the sunlight-the one I rarely got as a child, comes bursting forth, telling me it is a brand new day and that this time, the sun's vitamin D will revive my heart, soul and mind. My spirit is up to me.

And as I looked at the case study done and the psychology report that was done on me when I was about two years old, I read that I lacked a lot of vitamin D, I needed speech therapy and I needed to learn to form healthy attachments. But how could I if my a-mother told me that I was too fat and that I could not have that last piece of chicken?

When I was between 10 and 15 years old she insisted on serving my plate for me. The rest of the kids could serve their own, but I was not allowed to because I was "too fat." That marked the throw up days. Again, if I could not control the food put on my plate, I could at least control how much stayed in my system.

Throwing up made my cheeks sink in and I began to lose the weight my a-mother had told me I had. Keep in mind, I was 5'7, weighing 125 lbs..... but this was too fat for her. She was 5'4 weighing 110 lbs. and I had to be either her weight or less. I remember she told me one day "you look amazing M. What's your secret?"

I never told her I was throwing up.

My a-father did find out one day and he tried to help but my a-mother insisted that this made me look good....and that is what she wanted, for me to look good. It didn't matter that I was getting bad headaches and that I began throwing up water, and that my teeth were not looking right...as long as on the outside, I looked good and presentable, that was what mattered.

"They loved you. Look what they have done for you." That was always my favorite line from my white siblings who lived a lie. Everything was handed to them and they were also very smart. One never had to study at all, and the other was the one we went to because she was the bridge to my a-mother when I needed something. Whenever I asked, the answer was ALWAYS no. But when she asked, it was rare that she said NO. So I learned really quickly that I could never ask for anything unless it was through her.

They didn't love me. They loved the idea of me. When I was about 6 years old they decided to adopt more kids. My a-mother always said she adopted more kids "for me" because I was "having problems." But it was because they were getting so many positive comments about how saintly they were, they wanted to continue that pattern. I had no reason to believe they adopted for me. My a-mother was and still is self-centric and that won't change. She eventually adopted a special needs kid who she used against us when we were "bad."

I cut ties with my a-mother a few years back when she decided to read the 6% of my first book instead of the 100%. She was scanning for the parts where I talked poorly of her and didn't seem to care about the rest of my story, the part where abuse didn't keep me down. She hung on to that 6% and she has hated me ever since. One day she sent a damning letter to my workplace and put it in my mailbox. I had to tell my boss that she was no longer permitted on the premises. She told me that she was disowning me. She also told me that if I stepped foot on their property, that they would not hesitate to use their gun. Ha, (that is a nervous uncomfortable WTF laugh).

Yes, that is who she was and who she is today. A woman who I can't even call a mother.

"She never said that" my little white sister would tell me. Oh yes she did. "Show me" she would say. And no, I could not show her because I don't keep toxic things like that in my possession. I don't keep things telling me to go to hell in my possession. I can't find any sane reason to keep something that could destroy me, anywhere near me or my children.

But it is my truth! No one has the right to tell me that my truth is not valid.

The book I wrote is my truth. Only mine. I give no one else the ability to claim the truth that is who I am but is not who I will become.

So people, stop trying to tell adoptees what they did or did not experience, how they don't see things correctly, how their experiences are not real or valid. Stop doing this! Stop telling them to "watch their language" because it hurts your stupid little feelings. Stop trying to tell adoptees that they didn't have it that bad. Stop telling your children to smile if they don't feel like smiling. Stop telling your children that their feelings don't matter. Stop turning your adopted children into YOU because they are not you.

What we experience is our truth, and it belongs to no one else.

When Jesus talks about knowing the truth, He is not talking about him being the savior. He is talking about an experience the disciples were having. John 8:32-33. "if you continue in my word, then you are truly disciples of mine, and you will know the truth and the truth will set you free." The fact that he uses a conjunction here states that there are stipulations. When he says "continue" he means ongoing. This is an action; this is an experience the disciples are having that is going to bring them to an understanding that will create freedom for them. This is not about just blindly believing in Jesus; this is about a continued relationship with the experience they are having with this Jesus man.

In Greek, the word truth is the same as *reality, and knowledge*. The reality of the lived experience is what allows us to be free. What we know about our experience liberates us.

My first book was the start of my first truth. It helped me to cut ties and it has also given me a sense of freedom that no one else can give.

When we are true to our lived experience, and when we are no longer wearing the duct tape around our mouths and eyes and ears, we are able to open up an entirely new world where our lived experiences help shape us to be better people.

So stop telling us that what we experienced was not as....... we are not listening to you anymore.

Acknowledgements

I want to thank my editors for their time and dedication to this book. I'm aware that it was not an "easy" read and greatly appreciate all the feedback. I have also really enjoyed our conference time as we talked about this book and life in general. Thank you for giving me another day of joy!

Thank you: Sigrid F, Shannon H, Jill C, Sheryl T, Mary C, Debbie B, Jenny S, and Keeley R.

About the Author

Mae Claire is an author of three non-fiction books, one romance novel and one young adult novel. She translated the young adult novel into Spanish to help reach more people. All of the books draw from her experience as an adoptee.

In addition to being an author, Mae Claire is a teacher, adoption consultant, advocate for international adoptees in the United States and an adoptive parent. She is also an artist, jewelry-maker, singer, and avid chess player.

She lives in Massachusetts with her wife, daughter and neurotic dog.

References

Aidi, H. (2015). Haitians in the Dominican Republic in Legal Limbo. *Aljezeera*.

Green Card Process and Procedures. (2016, March 21). Retrieved from The Department of Homeland Security: https://www.uscis.gov/green-card/green-card-processes-and-procedures/green-card-processes-procedures

Hilpern, K. (2007, December 15). A different kind of love. *The Guardian*.

S.2275 - Adoptee Citizenship Act of 2015. (2016, March 21). Retrieved from Congress.gov: https://www.congress.gov/bill/114th-congress/senate-bill/2275

Made in the USA
Las Vegas, NV
07 October 2021